Table of Contents

Spanish:

Learn Spanish for Beginners in a Fun and Easy Way

Spanish Short Stories for Beginners:

21 Entertaining Short Stories to Learn Spanish and Develop Your Vocabulary the Fun Way!

Spanish:

Learn Spanish for Beginners in a Fun and Easy Way

Including Pronunciation, Spanish Grammar, Reading, and Writing, Plus Short Stories

By: University of Linguistics

Introduction

Welcome to "*Learn Spanish for Beginners in a Fun and Easy Way: Including Pronunciation, Spanish Grammar, Reading, and Writing, Plus Short Stories.*" In this book, we are going to jump right into the fundamentals of learning Spanish and how you can maximize your efforts.

If you are reading this, it is because you are keen on learning Spanish in the best possible way. This means that you are looking for the simplest and most effective way to learn one of the world's most important languages.

Of course, you could always sign up for a Spanish school in your city. Or, you could make an adventure out of it and travel to any one of the exotic countries in Latin America. You could even hire a private tutor to work with you on a one-on-one basis.

But let's face the fact that not everyone has the time to dedicate a fixed amount of their time to Spanish lessons. In fact, you might be so busy that just reading this requires you to clear up your schedule. That is why this guide has been designed to get your Spanish skills off the ground quickly and easily.

If you have tried to learn Spanish or another language the old-fashioned way, you can understand where this is coming from. It's not easy to take time out of your already packed schedule to go to class or work with a private tutor. Also, traveling to another country, while exciting, can take a good chunk out of your time, and it doesn't come cheap.

This guide will get you acquainted with the fundamentals of Spanish. You might be surprised to find that it is much easier to learn Spanish than you have initially thought. If you have struggled with it in the past, it is because you haven't found the right approach. That is the goal of this book. It is intended for those who want to maximize their efforts and talents.

In addition, Spanish is used by close to a billion native speakers and about another billion people as a second or third language, making it one of the most prominent languages in the West. As proof, it is among the six of United Nation's official languages.

Beyond that, learning Spanish will open doors to you into a world of culture, literature, and entertainment. Additionally, Latin America is a host to some of the most beautiful countries in the world. As such, these make great travel destinations at a surprisingly affordable price (when compared to traveling to Europe or Asia).

It is not hard to make a compelling case when it comes to the importance of learning Spanish. There are countless reasons that learning Spanish will improve your overall skillset even if you don't need it for work. Speaking multiple languages not only opens doors to other cultures but also has health benefits, such as improved cognition and concentration. Learning a second or third language has been linked to improved memory skills and heightened learning skills.

Plus, learning new languages can become one of those hobbies that just snowballs over time.

Why not?

If you have been thinking about taking up languages as a hobby or simply as a new challenge, then look no further. This guide, in addition to subsequent guides, will help you get on the road (and stay on it) to mastering a new language. You will feel satisfied with yourself and your accomplishments after you learn Spanish through this guide. The longer you wait, the more you are missing out on this wonderful experience.

Chapter 1: How to Learn a New Language

For most folks, learning a new language is one of the most challenging things they will ever do in their lives. The reason for this is that languages don't come easy. They take time and dedication for the learner to achieve a certain level of proficiency.

It takes several years of study and development before we can be reasonably proficient in a language. It is around the age of 7 or 8 when a child is able to communicate fairly well. Nevertheless, it takes a few more years of schooling and training before an individual truly masters a language. Even then, some folks are unable to go beyond a certain level of mastery.

The Advantage of Learning as an Adult

The big difference between learning a language as a child and learning a language as an adult lies in the fact that many of the cognitive processes, which children need to develop, have already been developed.

What does that mean?

It means that you don't need to go back and re-learn the alphabet or work on phonics. You can begin to reasonably decode a new language with some helpful pointers. Also, this means that you don't have to learn the mechanics of reading and writing. These are skills that you have already gotten a handle on in your native language.

So, what happens when you learn a new language is that you are transferring the skills you have already developed in your native language to the new language that you are learning. While that sounds rather straightforward, there are some bumps along the way.

First of all, language systems tend to vary significantly.

In general, languages function like complex systems that depend on logic. Every language has its own logic. However, that logic doesn't always make sense when compared to other languages. In fact, when you look at language, it is like getting a glimpse into the way the mind of people works.

Secondly, some languages share a common ancestry, while others have no relation between them, whatsoever. Most Indo-European languages share some kind of similarity among them. This can be observed in the syntax (word order) and the structure of words themselves. If this is the case, then it is a lot easier to make sense of the way such a language is structured.

Thirdly, some languages share a common base from which they splinter off into different directions. One such example is the so-called "romance languages." These languages share a common ancestry in the Latin spoken by the old Roman Empire. That common base can be seen in the syntax and similarity in roots and word families. Yet, the similarities pretty much end there. Each language (Spanish,

French, Italian, and so on) go off into their own direction, thus making them unique in their own right.

Main Differences Between English and Spanish

So, what can you do to make learning a new language easier on you?

Based on the previous examples, the first aspect to consider is syntax. In the case of English and Spanish, they both share common syntax insofar as the subject preceding the verb. Then, the object of the verb follows right after the verb. This basic structure is essentially the same. However, there are some subtle differences. For instance, adjectives precede nouns in Spanish, whereas the opposite is true in English.

Also, romance languages make use of gender-specific nouns. This is one of the most significant differences between English and Spanish. For example, Spanish has a specific gender assigned to all nouns in the language. Now, determining the gender for each noun depends on its spelling. A general rule of thumb, in this case, is that "o" ending nouns are treated as masculine nouns, while the feminine nouns are identified with "a" ending nouns. This is a general rule of thumb, and there are a number of exceptions. Nevertheless, it is a good standard to rely on.

There is also a far more complex verb conjugation system in Spanish than in English. The most complex verb conjugations in English can be found with irregular verbs in the past tense and the past participle form. Beyond that, verb conjugation is fairly self-explanatory in English.

In Spanish, though, verb conjugations are dependent on verb tense and the verb ending of the verb in its infinitive form. This difference can make conjugating verbs seem hard. But once you become familiar with the patterns for each type of verb, you will find it to be much easier than you had initially anticipated.

These three main differences make English rather different from Spanish and are the source of frustration for many Spanish learners. In this guide, we will not only focus on these differences but also on other insider tips that will surely help you gain an advantage in your endeavors with the Spanish language.

Now, here are some general guidelines that you can follow when learning Spanish.

- Listening practice is one of the most important exercises you can do on a regular basis. There are many audiovisual materials online. These materials will help you train your ear for the sound or the "music" of the Spanish language. In this case, you will not only hone your listening skills but also your pronunciation skills.
- Vocabulary lists are old-fashioned but still hold their merits. Now, we are not advocating that you make long lists of words and pound them into your mind. What we are saying is keep a journal of the language you learn on a daily basis. This journal can be something as simple as writing down new words and expressions you learn. You can use drawings, pictures, and notes to help you imprint their meanings in your mind.

- Grammar rules can be effective if that is something that you find useful. Not all people find grammar rules to be particularly useful and engaging. So, if you feel that writing out rules will help you fixate meaning in your mind, then, by all means, do so. If you don't feel too keen on memorizing rules, schematics, such as flowcharts and diagrams, can certainly help you gain a much different visual perspective.
- The use of translation is alright at the beginning. While you will hear some teachers say that translation will actually harm your development, it is worth mentioning that translation can help you navigate through the meaning of words and grammar in the very early stages of your development. Later on, translation can help you when you are traveling or interacting with other folks who may require your assistance.
- Watching movies and TV shows are a great source of language for you to learn. Also, music is a wonderful way to become close to the Spanish language. So, take a shot learning a song you like, or simply enjoying a telenovela. You will find that exposing yourself to Latin American culture from the get-go will pay off right away.

In the next chapter, we are going to take a look at the fundamental underpinnings of the Spanish language and how you can get a grip on the most important secrets to gain proficiency as a new Spanish speaker.

Chapter 2: The Fundamentals of Spanish

Spanish, like all languages, has its own nuances that make it truly unique. And while it shares common ancestry with French and Italian, Spanish does have its own characteristics, which can make it tricky for English speakers to master.

The great thing about learning languages nowadays is that we have been able to get to the root of how language systems work. This implies that you don't have to guess as to how a language works. That work has already been done for you. The endeavors of great linguists have led to a deep understanding of how languages work and how they can be learned.

That translates into a flattening of the curve for learners such as you. In the past, most language learners either needed to drill down and figure out how a language worked by themselves or just "go with the flow." The problem with either approach is that it doesn't allow you to gain a full appreciation of the way you can learn a language in an efficient manner.

That being said, Spanish is a rather straightforward language to learn. While it does have its intricacies, these are not as complex as you might think. As such, we will go over them in order to lay sound ground rules that can help you get your Spanish skills off the ground.

So, let us explore the fundamentals rules of the language and how they can be compared to the way English works. In this manner, you will be able to focus on the most troublesome areas that English speakers have when learning Spanish.

Male-Female Agreement

The first thing that jumps out at English speakers is the use of the male-female agreement. This characteristic of Spanish is quite different from English, considering the fact that English is a gender-neutral language. As such, getting used to the male-female agreement is a bit challenging early on.

The main rule of thumb for the male-female agreement is based on observing the spelling of the noun in question. Initially, the article attached to the noun will be your first clue. So, if the article preceding a noun is "el," then it's masculine. It the article preceding the noun is "la," then it is feminine.

However, what happens if you do have the article? Then you must rely on the spelling of the word. As we have mentioned before, "-o" ending nouns are masculine, and "-a" ending nouns are must be treated as feminine. For example, "toro" (bull) is masculine. So, you would express it as "el toro" (the bull). In the case of "vaca" (cow), it is considered feminine. So, you would express it as "la vaca" (the cow).

These examples make a clear point of how you can use the "o" and "a" rule to give you a heads up on the gender of a noun.

Verb Conjugation

Another important rule to consider in Spanish is verb conjugation. Now, conjugation may seem a bit tricky, but it is not quite as tough as it seems.

The foundation for verb conjugation depends on the ending of the infinitive form of the verb. There are three types of endings for the infinitive form of verbs: AR, ER, and IR.

Based on these endings, you will find that they can be conjugated in either the past, present, or future forms. Here are some examples of verbs in the infinitive form based on their endings:

Verbs ending in "AR" are as follows:

- Jugar (to play)
- Saltar (to jump)
- Cantar (to sing)
- Volar (to fly)
- Mirar (to look)

Verbs ending in "ER" are as follows:

- Comer (to eat)
- Volver (to return)
- Aprender (to learn)
- Entender (to understand)
- Acceder (to access)

"IR" ending verbs:

- Sentir (to feel)
- Transmitir (to transmit)
- Abrir (to open)
- Corregir (to correct)
- Permitir (to permit)

As you can see, all Spanish verbs in their infinitive form will all fall into one of these three groups. Later on, we will discuss verb conjugation in depth. We have an entire chapter devoted to verb conjugation. In this chapter, you will see how straightforward verb conjugation can be in Spanish.

Adjectives in Singular and Plural

Another potentially complex aspect of Spanish grammar is the singular and plural form of adjectives. The general rule in English is that adjectives do not have a plural form. In Spanish, adjectives not only agree in terms of male and female but also singular and plural.

A great example of this form can be seen in colors. Colors must agree in terms of both color and quantity. Let's use "azul" (blue) as an example. So, "ojos azules" (blue eyes) agree both in terms of gender ("ojos" is male) and number ("azules" is plural). This exemplifies how it is important to make sure that adjectives agree with the subject of the sentence, both in terms of gender and number.

On the subject of nouns and adjectives, in English, adjectives precede nouns. In Spanish, it is the opposite. For instance, "zapatos negros" (black shoes) agrees both in terms of gender and number. But you can also see how the noun comes before the color. This is an important difference, but it's an easy one to remember, as it is just essentially the opposite of the word order used in English.

Sentences Without Subject

One other important nuance of Spanish that is shared among the romance languages is that the subject of the sentence isn't always needed. What that means is that the subject of the verb can be omitted in cases where it is absolutely clear what the subject is or if it can be inferred what the subject is.

Let's consider this example: "soy de Inglaterra" (I am from England). Notice that the subject "yo" (I) is not included as the verb "soy" (am), which makes it perfectly clear that you are referring to yourself. As such, the subject can be omitted since it can be easily inferred whom you are talking about. In those cases, when there are references to multiple people and objects, omitting the subject can lead to confusion. Consequently, you might have to ask for clarification or even offer it in order to make sure no information gets lost along the way.

In the following chapters, we will be taking a look at these and other equally important aspects of Spanish at great length. So, buckle up because we are going for quite a ride.

Chapter 3: Basic Spanish Words and Phrases

When starting out with Spanish, you definitely need to get some basic words and phrases so that you can communicate with the people you meet and interact with in common social settings, such as restaurants, airports, bars, or any other places.

That is why we are going to take a look at some words and phrases that you can use right out of the box. Most importantly, they will be able to help you make the most of your social interactions when you travel or find yourself in a group of Spanish speakers. Moreover, these expressions can also help you when you find yourself in a business context with Spanish speakers.

Greetings

First of all, greetings are essential. Consider these:

- Buenos días (good morning)
- Buenas tardes (good afternoon)
- Buenas noches (goodnight / good evening)

There are three simple greetings that you can use to greet other folks when you see them. The rule of thumb is that any time before noon is considered to be "buenos días." Starting at noon, the greeting switches to "buenas tardes." Then, as soon as it gets dark, the greeting switches to "buenas noches."

Also, notice that there is no "good evening" in Spanish. That is why any time it is dark, you would use the "buenas noches" greeting. We will be covering this particular point in greater depth in the chapter regarding time.

It should also be noted that when you are greeting people after midnight, "buenas noches" applies if you still have not gone to bed. However, if you are getting up very early in the morning, then the greeting switches to "buenos días" since you are starting out your day.

For instance, if you are returning from a party at two o'clock in the morning, your greeting would be buenas noches as you still haven't gone to bed. By the same token, if you are rising at two o'clock in the morning, that is, your day is starting out, then you may greet folks as "buenos días."

When greeting people, the traditional "hola" (hello) can't go wrong. This is a universal way in which you can greet people in Spanish. It can be used in both formal and informal contexts. You can combine it as "hola, buenos días" (hello, good morning), and you instantly have the means to approach anyone, especially strangers, in public settings.

Here are some expressions which you can use to ask people how they are doing:

- ¿Qué haces? (What are you doing?)
- ¿Cómo está usted? (How are you?) – formal
- ¿Qué pasa? (What's happening?)

- ¿Cómo estás? (How are you?) – informal
- ¿Qué tal? (What's up?)
- ¿Qué onda? (What's up?) – very informal

These expressions are all variations of "how are you?" though the difference lies in the level of formality, which they represent.

Also, you can use the following expressions to respond to these greetings.

- Bien, gracias. (Good, thank you)
- Muy bien. (Very well)
- Más o menos. (so-so)

These responses are all typical and can be used in any situation. If you happen to be feeling unwell, you could use an expression, such as "no me siento bien" (I feel unwell), especially if you are being asked by the medical staff.

You can follow greetings with:

- ¿Y usted? (and you?) – formal
- ¿Y tú? (and you?)– informal

So, you might have a conversation such as this:

- Hola, buenos días. ¿Cómo estás?
  - Bien gracias, ¿y tú?
- Muy bien, gracias.

This brief exchange illustrates how these expressions can be used to greet a person in virtually any type of context.

Introductions

When introducing yourself, you can use the following to indicate your name:

- Mi nombre es________. (My name is_______.)
- Me llamo ______. (My name is________.)

Both expressions are used to state your name, though "me llamo" literally means, "I am called." However, the meaning of this phrase is "my name is..."

To ask for a person's name, you can use the following:

- Formal: ¿Cuál es su nombre? (What is your name?)
- Informal: ¿Cómo te llamas? (What is your name?)

Both questions are asking the person to indicate their name, though the latter literally means "what are you called?" Nevertheless, both questions are asking for the person's name. The response could be either "Me llamo..." or "Mi nombre es..."

Another great expression which you can use when introducing yourself is: "soy de..." (I am from...)

For example, you can say, "Soy de una gran ciudad en los Estados Unidos." (I am from a large city in the United States.). All you need to do in this case is insert the name of your country or city so that your interlocutors know where you are from.

Common Expressions and Questions

Here are some more essential Spanish expressions:

- Aqui tiene (here you go)
- De nada (you're welcome)
- Disculpe (excuse me)
- Lo siento (I'm sorry)
- Muchas gracias (Thank you very much)
- Perdón (pardon, though it can also be used as "excuse me")
- Gracias (Thank you)
- Por favor (please)

These expressions will certainly come in handy when you are traveling through airports, going to restaurants, or interacting with folks in public places, such as offices, shops, or hotels. Also, they are universal and polite, and they work well in any Spanish-speaking country.

Now, let's take a look at some questions that can be used in a variety of situations:

- ¿Cuánto cuesta esto? (How much is this?)
- ¿Puede ayudarme? (Can you help me?)
- ¿De dónde eres? (Where are you from?)
- ¿Dónde vives? (Where do you live?)
- ¿Dónde está______? (Where is______?)
- ¿Qué hora es? (What time is it?)
- ¿Dónde puedo encontrar un taxi?) (Where can I find a taxi?)
- ¿Puede hablar más despacio? (Can you speak slower?)
- ¿Puedo ayudarle? (Can I help you?)
- ¿Puede repetir, por favor? (Can you repeat, please?)
- ¿Qué significa_______? (What does______ mean?)

The questions above are all great for socializing and getting to know other folks. Plus, you can use them in virtually any type of social setting, from an informal gathering to a formal business meeting. You can make them more polite by adding "por favor."

Here are some other great expressions that will surely come in handy at any time.

- Claro (of course)
- Estoy perdido (I am lost)
- Hablo poco español (I speak a little Spanish)
- No (no)
- No entiendo (I don't understand)
- No sé (I don't know)
- No tengo idea (I don't have any idea)

- Nunca (never)
- Sí (yes)
- Siempre (always)
- Sin problema (no problem)
- Tal vez (perhaps)

All of these expressions are good for getting around in Spanish-speaking countries. They can help you navigate the situations in which you find yourself.

Now, let's look at some expressions which you can use on various occasions.

- ¡Salud! (cheers)
- Bienvenido (welcome, singular)
- Bienvenidos (welcome, plural)
- Buen provecho (bon appetit)
- Felicitaciones (congratulations)
- Feliz cumpleaños (happy birthday)
- Qué la pase bien (hope you have a good time)

These expressions are used in various social situations. Perhaps the most uncommon expression for English speakers is "buen provecho." This expression is used when sitting down at the table before eating and then again upon leaving the table after a meal. It basically means "have a good meal," and its closest equivalent would be "bon appetite." Don't be surprised if you hear this expression when eating. You can simply reply with "buen provecho" any time you hear it directed at you.

Lastly, let's take a look at some expressions that we can use to say goodbye:

- Adiós (goodbye)
- Hasta luego (see you later)
- Cuídate (take care)
- Hasta mañana (see you tomorrow)
- Buen viaje (have a good trip)
- Tenga buen día (have a nice day, formal)
- Nos vemos (see you, very informal)
- Tenga buena noche (have a good night)

As you can see, these expressions can be used to take your leave. They vary in formality, though you could combine "nos vemos" with a specific time or date at the end of a business meeting. For example, "nos vemos la próxima semana" (see you next week) can be used to indicate that you will have another meeting next week.

By now, you have enough tools to get around Spanish-speaking countries. That way, you will know what to respond in virtually any situation and circumstances. Best of all, you will be both polite and friendly. You can't go wrong with that!

Chapter 4: The Alphabet

The alphabet used in Spanish is exactly the same as the one in English. This is the Latin alphabet and contains no variations when compared to the English character set. This makes it very easy to identify letters and words in Spanish. Pronunciation, however, is a different story.

The Spanish character set contains the same 26 letters used in English, plus an additional character known as "ñ" (pronounced /enyeh/). This is an additional character, which is essentially exclusive to Spanish. The accent atop the "n" is called "vergulilla." It is only used on the "n" to form the "ñ," and it is not used on vowels such as the case of Portuguese.

Recently, the Real Academia Española – RAE - (Royal Spanish Academy) dropped the official recognition of the letters "ch," "rr," and "ll." These double consonants were previously considered to be letters in their own right, given the spelling of some words. However, the RAE deemed them not to be letters. So, the sounds they produce are the result of a consonant combination and not the product of an individual letter.

The Spanish Character Set

First, let us examine the Spanish character set below:

Aa /ah/	Bb /beh/	Cc /seh/	Dd /deh/	Ee /eh/	Ff /efeh/
Gg /heh/	Hh /acheh/	Ii /ee/	Jj /hota/	Kk /kah/	Ll /eleh/
Mm /emeh/	Nn /eneh/	Ññ /enyeh/	Oo /oh/	Pp /peh/	Qq /kooh/
Rr /ereh/	Ss /eseh/	Tt /teh/	Uu /ooh/	Vv /veh/	Ww /doble ooh/
Xx /ehkees/	Yy /ee greeahguh/	Zz /zehtah/			

Table 1. The Spanish alphabet

The figure above presents the full character set for the Spanish alphabet. As you can see, the only character not present in the English language is the "ñ." The significant variation between the two alphabets lies in the pronunciation of each letter.

Another similarity between English and Spanish is the use of the same designation of characters for vowel sounds. The traditional A, E, I, O, U letters are used to represent vowel sounds. Given the phonetic construction of Spanish, there are only five vowel sounds and a combination of diphthongs and triphthongs. There are also no long nor short sounds like in English. Overall, there are 14 vowel sounds in English as compared to the five basic sounds in Spanish. It should be noted that whenever there is a combination of vowels written together, they must all be pronounced individually. For example, in "día" (day), the "ee-ah" vowels are pronounced together. This is important to keep in mind, especially if you are used to French where multiple vowels combine to form one sound.

As for the consonants, each letter has its own individual sound. When combined, the sound of each letter must be pronounced just as with vowels. There are a couple of exceptions, however.

First, the double "L" combination makes a "y" sound. For instance, "Lluvia" is not pronounced as /lloveeah/ but rather /youveeah/. As mentioned earlier, the "ll" combination was once considered to be an individual letter but has recently been changed by the RAE.

The same goes for the use or "rr." For example, "guardarropa" (wardrobe) would be considered "rr" as an individual letter. Since the RAE no longer recognizes "rr" as a letter, the pronunciation of the word remains the same, but the official spelling of the word is officially "r-r" as opposed to "rr."

One other letter that is no longer recognized by the RAE is "ch." This letter is now the "c-h" combination as opposed to the former "ch."

Now, let's take a look at pronunciation.

Pronunciation Differences

In general, Spanish is a very easy language to read since each letter represents one sound and must be pronounced as such. In other words, Spanish is read and pronounced exactly as it is spelled. This is one clear advantage that Spanish has over other languages.

Nevertheless, there are some phonological differences between English and Spanish.

The first and perhaps the most obvious is the "rolling R." The rolling Rs tend to give native English speakers a hard time. Perhaps the best comparison of this sound can be found in the Irish accent. The rolling R in the Irish accent is actually quite similar to the one in Spanish. Of course, it takes some time and practice. But given time, you, too, can learn to pronounce it appropriately.

Another key difference lies in the pronunciation of "Q." In English, words with "Q,"such as "quick," are pronounced as /kwik/. In Spanish though, they are pronounced as /k/. For instance, "queso" (cheese) is not pronounced as /kwehsoh/ but as /kehsoh/.

This is a very significant difference as it can lead to some miscommunication both when listening and speaking. Sure, it may not derail meaning altogether, but it will make it somewhat difficult to get the message across.

Then, there is the matter of the silent "H." This letter is never pronounced in Spanish, though it is used in writing. So, "hotel" would not be /hotel/ but /ohtel/. This is a very straightforward rule. So, please don't pronounce the "h" whenever you see it printed.

The "G" and "J" can be somewhat confusing. They both produce the /h/ sound depending on the vowel combination. Now, "J" is easy as it will always produce the /h/ sound. The difference lies with "G." In the combinations "GE" and "GI," the sound is /heh/ and /hee/. For example, "general" would be pronounced as /hehneral/ and "giro" (turn) would be /heeroh/. In the case of "GA," "GO," and "GU," the soft /g/ sound is produced. For instance, "gato" (cat) would be /gahtoh/, "golf" would be /gohlf/, and "gustar" (like) would be /goostoh/. Please bear these differences in mind when reading through Spanish text and when pronouncing words.

The last point on pronouncing letters lies with "B" and "V." In European Spanish, both letters sound the same as their English counterparts. However, in Latin American Spanish, both letters sound exactly the same; that is, they have the same bilabial /b/ sound. So, "botar" (drop) and "votar" (vote) both sound the same /bohtahr/. Since they are both indistinguishable, it is up to you to recognize the context where the words are used. That will give you enough reference to determine which word is being said.

On the whole, the Spanish alphabet is pretty straightforward. This is certainly an advantage for native speakers of English or any other romance language. Do take the time to go over each letter and its pronunciation. You will soon find that they are not as hard as you might have thought.

Chapter 5: Pronunciation

Spanish pronunciation has its intricacies as all languages do. On the whole, the overall sound of the language is a lot softer when compared to other languages, such as eastern European or Asian languages. What this means is that most of the sounds are articulated in the higher part of the throat.

Also, the tongue plays a vital role in articulating sounds properly. This is especially true in the case of the rolling Rs. For most English speakers, the rolling Rs tend to be quite a bit of a challenge. Nevertheless, with some practice and dedication, clear pronunciation can be achieved.

Another important aspect of Spanish phonetics is that all vowels must be pronounced individually. The only combination of vowels occurs with the "gu" and "qu" combination. For example, "guerra" does not require the "u" to be pronounced as in /gwerra/. Rather, the pronunciation is similar to /gerra/.

Diphthongs & Triphthongs

Now, one of the things that tends to be somewhat tricky early on is the pronunciation of several vowels in a word. When you have two vowel sounds in succession, you are pronouncing a "diphthong." When you have three sounds, this is called a "triphthong."

Diphthongs are quite common in Spanish. For example, the "ía" ending used in the habitual past is pronounced as /ee-ah/. So, words such as "corría" /koh-ree-ah/ (would run) or "comía" /koh-mee-ah/ (would eat) are good examples of diphthongs.

Here are some examples of diphthongs in Spanish:

- Aire
- Automóvil
- bailar
- Oigo
- Prisionero

As you become more and more familiar with the way Spanish is pronounced, you will find that diphthongs are actually quite easy to identify and pronounce. So, do take the time to go over these items.

With regard to triphthongs, these can be a bit tricky, especially since they aren't that common in English. For instance, "hour," "flour," "fire," and "dire" illustrate the way in which you can pronounce three vowel sounds in a single word. "Flour" /flow-ooh-uhr/ has three sounds, though native speakers tend to reduce the overall sound down to two. This can be quite tricky for English learners, as they might have some difficulty pronouncing these sounds. Luckily for them, triphthongs aren't nearly as prevalent in English as they are in Spanish.

Here as some examples of triphthongs in Spanish:

- Bioinformática
- Buey
- Cambiáis
- Semiautomático
- Uruguay

Just like in the case of English, most native Spanish speakers will reduce these sounds in order to suit their accent best. As such, you might not be able to pick up on the individual sounds quite easily at first. Nevertheless, as you gain more practice with them, you will be able to clearly hear the various sounds in action.

Consonant Sounds

As far as consonants go, these tend to be articulated much the same way as English, though they are "softer" than their English counterparts. For example, /t/ does not have the same hard sound, especially at the end of the word. So, "importante" /im-por-tahn-teh/ has a "softer" sound in both "Ts." The hard sounding "T," as well as "R" is a dead giveaway that your first language is English.

Consequently, the best way for you to pick up on the correct pronunciation of Spanish vowels and consonants is to practice listening as much as you can. The best thing about listening is that you can pick up the way native Spanish speakers utter the various consonant sounds.

Now, here's a couple of interesting points about consonant sounds in Spanish.

First, bear in mind that the /v/ and /b/ sounds have no distinction in Latin American accents. While European Spanish speakers do make this differentiation, Latinos won't. So, you might get crossed up with some of the words being spoken. In addition, the /f/ and /v/ sounds, while articulated in English in the same way, are dissimilar in Spanish.

The same goes for the /s/ and /z/ sounds. Both of these sounds are identical in Latin American Spanish. For instance, "zapato" (shoe) would be pronounced with an /s/ sound as in /sapato/ as opposed to the /z/ sound. As an English speaker, you can certainly use the /z/ with any word that contains the letter "z." However, bear in mind that Latinos won't make this distinction.

The letter "z" does prove to be a bit of a curveball in European Spanish. In European Spanish, the /z/ sound is more similar to using the "th" letter combination in English. As such, "zapato" would sound more like /thahpahto/. While there really isn't anything wrong with either pronunciation style, it all boils down to your ability to pick up on these differences when hearing other speakers.

Another consonant combination to keep in mind are the "sh" and "ch" combinations. For instance, "chocolate" would be /choh-koh-lah-the/ (notice how each set of vowels is pronounced). However, the "sh" sound isn't native to Spanish. In fact, the sound exists because it has been imported from other languages. For example, "show" and "flash" have been imported directly from English. This is evident in the fact that a word such as "desahcer" (undo) would be pronounced as

/dehs-ah-sehr/ and not /desh-ah-ser/. So, while Spanish speakers do utilize the sound, it is not inherent to the language. Rather, it has been imported from other languages.

At this point, it is worth mentioning that Spanish pronunciation is quite straightforward once you get the hang of the individual sounds that comprise it. While you may struggle somewhat with the various accent variations from country to country, it is worth noting that the more time you spend in a single country, the more familiar you will become with that accent.

Think about it this way. Imagine English learners learning English in Scotland and then moving to Australia.

These differences can be tough at first. Hence, it is recommended that you focus on the accent of the region that you are going to visit. So, if you are planning to travel to Mexico, try your best to become familiar with the Mexican accent. If you are looking to travel to Colombia, then becoming familiar with the Colombian accent is a must. The best part of all is that websites such as YouTube are filled with videos and tutorials on the various Latin American accents.

Here's one final note: you will hear newscasters use a flatter, more neutral accent. This is intended to reduce the amount of confusion that may arise from one regional accent to another. As such, this type of accent is the kind that you can shoot for in order to help yourself be understood everywhere you go.

Chapter 6: Syllabication

Syllabication is the separation of words into smaller units based on the sounds that are produced. In general, a syllable will consist of a vowel and consonant sound. Sometimes, syllables can be individual vowel sounds, though they are never individual consonant sounds.

When looking at the way syllables are formed in all languages, these tend to break down based on the natural phonological patterns of that language. Nevertheless, the vowel-consonant connection is common throughout virtually all languages.

It is generally accepted that early human language was monosyllabic; that is, early human communication was done through the utterance of individual sounds. To this day, we still use monosyllabic communication to convey meaning. For example, expressions such as "huh" can be used to indicate a specific meaning. Other essential words in English, like "yes" and "no" are classic examples of monosyllabic communication.

With the evolution of human language, communication became more and more complex. This led to the union of individual sounds in order to form words. Now, it should be noted that monosyllabic utterances are also words (such as "I"). Nevertheless, these are generally considered to be isolated sounds. This is especially true when these isolated sounds do not actually have any meaning attached to them.

As human communication becomes richer, the need for more and more words led to the use of syllables under various combinations. This is the reason that one of the most effective methods used to teach kids how to read is based on phonics.

Phonics is composed of core sounds; when combined, they can produce a myriad of words. Consequently, phonics, as individual syllables, can be used to make words. At the end of the day, the words that we use in daily conversation are nothing more than the aggregate of any number of syllable combinations.

Spanish is no exception to this evolution. Children in Spanish schools are taught to read and write using these basic building blocks of language. Initially, children learn the five-vowel sounds before moving on to isolated consonant sounds. Then, vowels sounds are tacked on to individual consonant sounds. For example, children are taught to read, "ma," "me," "mi," "mo," "mu." These syllables, in themselves, are meaningless. However, when they are combined with other such combinations, they can lead to word formation.

Let's take a quick look at how these syllables can be used to make words. For instance, "mama" is one of the first words children in Spanish schools begin to read. So, just like children in English schools learn to read English and pronounce it correctly using phonics, children in Spanish schools use these segregated syllables to make their first words.

Syllabication Structure

As such, each consonant is combined with the five vowel sounds to produce words. Let's take a closer look at this syllabication structure:

- Ba, be, bi, bo, bu
- Ca, ce, ci, co, cu
- Da, de, di, do, du
- fa, fe, fi, fo, fu
- ga, ge, gi, go, gu
- ha, he, hi, ho, hu
- ja, je, ji, jo, ju
- ka, ke, ki, ko, ku
- la, le, li, lo, lu
- ma, me, mi, mo, mu
- na, ne, ni, no, un
- ña, ñe, ñi, ño, ñu
- pa, pe, pi, po, pu
- ra, re, ri, ro, ru
- sa, se, si, so, su
- ta, te, ti, to, tu
- va, ve, vi, vo, vu
- wa, we, wi, wo, wu
- ya, ye, yi, yo, yu
- za, ze, zi, zo, zu

The two letters that are excluded from this list are "Q," as it is always combined with "U" and produce a /k/ sound, and "X" which is not used at the beginning of words. In fact, there are a few exceptions, such as "xilófono" (xylophone), where it is used at the beginning of a word.

From here onward, you can combine any number of these syllables to make your own words. Consider this:

- ma + pa = mapa (map)
- ro + sa = rosa (rose)
- ta + za = taza (cup)
- ca + ma = cama (bed)
- tu + yo = tuyo (yours)

These are two-syllable words. And then here are some three-syllable words:

- to + ma + tc = tomatc (tomato)
- pa + ta + ta = patata (potato)
- ta + ja + da = tajada (slice)
- pa + pa + ya = papaya (papaya)
- ba + ti + do = batido (smoothie)

As you can see, Spanish is built on these individual syllable combinations. As you become more familiar with the language, you will see that all words can be broken down into these consonant-syllable units. This will make reading far easier while helping you get a grip on the proper pronunciation of the words.

The best way to go about your understanding of syllabication in Spanish is to repeat the various consonant-vowel combinations until you are able to begin forming your own words. At first, you'll have a list of two-syllable words. Then, you will begin to recognize three-syllable words, then four, and so on.

A word of caution: by now, you may have noticed that some words have an accent on them. As such, it is important to note that an accent indicates that the syllable is to be stressed. If there is no accent used in a word, then you will have to listen to the way it is pronounced.

Later on, we will be taking an in-depth look into the way accents are used in Spanish. But for now, it is important to be on the lookout for these accents. These will give you a clear indication as to how a word is pronounced.

And if you are ever in doubt with regard to the pronunciation of a word, tools such as spanishdict.com and Wordreference will help you get the right pronunciation. Best of all, you will be able to hear the way a word is pronounced in various Spanish accents. This is certainly an educational tool that will help you get it right every single time.

Chapter 7: Stress and Accents

In the previous chapter, we focused on syllabication of Spanish words. In that chapter, we mentioned the use of accents in Spanish as a means of indicating word stress.

But before we move on to the use of accents, let's establish what we mean by "stress." Stress refers to the syllable where a word receives its inflection. This inflection is what makes the word sound logical in a given language.

Consider this example:

The word, "chocolate" in English would be pronounced as CHOcolate. In this case, notice how the first syllable receives the stress. The same word, "chocolate" in Spanish, would be pronounced as chocoLAte. Please notice how the third syllable is the one that receives the stress. This is why you often hear Spanish speakers stress words incorrectly in English. While this won't necessarily hinder communication, it may lead to misunderstandings at some point.

Now that we have defined what stress is, there are some ground rules to the use of accents in Spanish.

Accent Types

First, there are three accent types. The first is known as "tilde." The tilde is used exclusively on vowels. It can be used to indicate that the syllable is to be stressed. For example, "comunicación" (communication) ought to be pronounced as comunicaCIÓN. Hence, the stress is placed on the last syllable.

Next, the other type of accent used on vowels is called a "diérisis" (dieresis). This accent mark is used exclusively in the "gu" combination. It is a bit of a rarity in Spanish, but it is present in some very common words. For example, "pingüino" (penguin) and "bilingüe" (bilingual) use this accent mark.

The reason for the use of the dieresis lies in the fact that the "gu" combination with other vowels produces a hard sound. For instance, "guerra" (war) is pronounced as /geh-rah/. However, if the dieresis is used as "güerra," then you would have a soft sound like /gweh-rah/. Needless to say, "güerra" does not exist in Spanish. Nevertheless, the use of the accent makes all the difference between the right word and a funky sounding mistake.

It is unclear as to how the dieresis came about in Spanish. Nevertheless, it is utilized in other languages. So, if you happen to be familiar with these accents in other languages, then you shouldn't be entirely surprised by their inclusion in Spanish.

The third type of accent is the "vergulilla." This is the accent above the "ñ." This is the only accent used on a consonant in Spanish. No other consonant has an accent placed on it. As noted earlier, the /en-yeh/ sound clear differentiates it from the /n/ sound. Just like the dieresis, it is unclear as to how the "ñ" emerged in Spanish.

It is widely accepted as a part of countless numbers of accents that were initially used in Spanish writing. Over time, Spanish writing was simplified, leaving the "ñ" on the books for practical reasons.

Uses of the Tilde

As you dig deeper into your Spanish studies, you will find that there are some rather complex orthographic rules that go into the use of Spanish. With the intent of simplifying things, we have compiled a list of cases where the use of the tilde is certain.

- Words that end in "ción" and "sión" will always carry a tilde on the "o." Examples are "conclusión" and "confirmación." Leaving the tilde off is considered to be a spelling mistake in this case.
- Verbs in the past tense, such as "jugué" (I played) and "dormí" (I slept) are good examples. Virtually, all verbs in the past tense will end in a tilde on the final consonant. This is a phonological device used to highlight clearly the tense of the verb.
- Verbs with the "ía" ending are another example. These verbs are roughly equivalent to the "would + verb" combination in English. For instance, "jugaría" (would play) and "dormía" (would sleep) are solid examples.
- Next, a verb in the future simple will also have a tilde on the final syllable. For example, "jugaré" (I will play) and "dormiré" (I will sleep) highlight this type of verb conjugation. Nevertheless, keep in mind that while "jugué" and "dormiré" both end in the same "é" vowel, they are completely different tenses.
- Then, there are "long" words that carry tildes in the middle of the word. These "long" words carry a tilde since they have more than four syllables. As such, the tilde is needed in order to guide the reader as to the proper pronunciation of the word. For instance, "demostrándole" (showing him) or "insertándolos" (inserting them) are words which could potentially be confusing if they didn't have the accent attached to them.
- Most words that carry the stress on the final syllable have a tilde on that syllable. This is intended to avoid any potential confusion in the word's pronunciation. Some examples include, "bebé" (baby), japonés (Japanese), "maíz) (maize, corn). On that note, nationalities that end in "nés" will always carry a tilde. By the way, nationalities are not capitalized in Spanish. Of course, not every single word that carries the stress in the final syllable has a tilde, but this is a good, general rule of thumb.
- Be on the lookout for names and surnames that carry a tilde. In legal terms, it is not required for names to carry tilde unless they are legally spelled that way. For instance, "Fernández" and "Fernandez" would be pronounced the same, though legally, it may be spelled without the tilde. This could be due to a clerical error. So, keep in mind that if an accentuated name or surname is spelled without the mark, it could be due to a legal issue.

The official ruling body on the use of tildes is the RAE. What this means is that if you are ever in doubt with the use of a tilde, there is the place where you can go. In general, the RAE dictionary is the official sources whenever you have any doubt on the spelling of a word of the conjugation of a verb. So, it certainly pays to keep this in mind.

Perhaps the best way to improve your use of accents is through reading. The more you read, the more you will notice which words carry an accent and which ones do not. This will allow you to become more familiar with the way that Spanish accents work.

At the end of the day, proper spelling and accentuation can be learned through constant practice. The guidelines in this chapter are meant to make the entire process as simple as possible. So now it's just a matter of practicing these points so that you can make the most of your practice time.

Chapter 8: The Use of Numbers, Colors, Time and Feelings

Counting in Spanish

Let's begin this chapter with the use of numbers. The number system in Spanish is based on a ten base (other languages, such as French, use numbers on a sixty base). This makes the numerical structure of Spanish rather similar to English. The first twenty digits are unique. After twenty, numbers all follow the same pattern until reaching one-hundred. After one-hundred, the same pattern repeats over and over until reaching one-thousand.

Let's have a look at the first ten numbers, including zero.

Spanish	**English**
0 = cero	Zero
1 = uno	One
2 = dos	Two
3 = tres	Three
4 = cuatro	Four
5 = cinco	Five
6 = seis	Six
7 = siete	Seven
8 = ocho	Eight
9 = nueve	Nine
10 = diez	Ten

Table 2. Numbers from 0 to 10 in Spanish

The first ten digits, plus zero, don't bear much resemblance to each other,though they are structured in the same manner. So, it is a matter of learning each digit accordingly. Arabic numbers are also used. Consequently, there is no problem in expressing numbers in the same manner.

Numbers eleven to twenty in Spanish words are presented in Table 3.

Spanish	English
11 = once	Eleven
12 = twelve	Doce
13 = trece	Thirteen
14 = catorce	Fourteen
15 = quince	Fifteen
16 = dieciseis	Sixteen
17 = diecisiete	Seventeen
18 = dieciocho	Eighteen
19 = diecinueve	Nineteen
20 = veinte	twenty

Table 3. Numbers from 11 to 20 in Spanish

In this list, you can see how each number is spelled out to reflect its combination of digits. In the case of dieciseis, deicisiete, dieciocho, and diecinueve, you may find that these are spelled as "diez y seis" (ten and six), "diez y siete" (ten and seven), "diez y ocho" (ten and eight), and "diez y nueve" (ten and nine). These are accepted spellings, though they are not usually taught that way. The reason for this is based on a simplified system where remembering the correct spelling of these numbers is a lot easier that way. Nevertheless, you can spell these numbers both ways, which should not make a difference.

One important pronunciation note is that "quince" (15) is pronounced as /keen-seh/ and not /kwIns/. So please keep this in mind whenever you are referring to this number.

Next, the numbers for twenty to thirty still have their own particular spelling. Let's have a look.

Spanish	English
21 = veintiuno	Twenty-one
22 = veintidós	Twenty-two
23 = veintitrés	Twenty-three
24 = veinticuatro	Twenty-four
25 = venticinco	Twenty-five
26 = veintiseis	Twenty-six
27 = veintisiete	Twenty-seven
28 = veintiocho	Twenty-eight
29 = veintinueve	Twenty-nine
30 = treinta	thirty

Table 4. Numbers from 21 to 30 in Spanish

With this lot of numbers, you will find that they have a specific spelling. Nevertheless, it is accepted to spell them as "veinte y uno," "veinte y dos," and so on. Ultimately, it is up to you to find the form that is much easier for you. Also, note that "veintidós" and "veintitrés" carry a tilde for you to recognize the stress on the word's last syllable.

The remaining numbers from 30 onward can be spelled as "treinta y uno" and so on. This makes it rather easy to spell out the remaining numbers up to one-hundred. Here is a list of the remaining numbers in order of tens.

Spanish	English
40 = cuarenta	Forty
50 = cincuenta	Fifty
60 = sesenta	Sixty
70 = setenta	Seventy
80 = ochenta	Eighty
90 = noventa	Ninety
100 = cien	One hundred
200 = doscientos	Two hundred
300 = trescientos	Three hundred
1000 = mil	One thousand

Table 5. Numbers from 40 to 1000 in Spanish

In this chart, you will notice how each ten is based on a single digit. So, "cuatro" becomes "cuarenta" and so on. Also, one hundred is spelled out as "cien." However, when combined with the remaining digits, the numbers would work out a "ciento uno" (101), "ciento dos" (102), and so on. What this means is that you can combine "ciento" with any other number. As such, "ciento treinta y nueve" (139) can be spelled out just like the earlier ones.

Also, "mil" is one thousand and can be combined as follows:

- Diez mil (ten thousand)
- Cien mil (one-hundred thousand)
- Un millón (one million)
- Diez millones (ten million)
- Mil millones (one billion)

Notice how "billion" is expressed as a "thousand million," though it is possible to say "un billon." Both forms would be understood, though "thousand million" would be more suitable for a formal business context.

Describing With Colors

Next, we have colors. One very important note about numbers is that, like all adjectives, colors are subject to the masculine-feminine agreement, as well as singular and plural agreement. This means that you need to make sure that the color agrees with the subject you are talking about.

First, let's have a list of the most commonly used colors.

Spanish	English
Amarillo	Yellow
Anaranjado	Orange
Azul	Blue
Blanco	White
Gris	Grey
Marron	Brown
Morado	Purple
Negro	Black
Rojo	Red
Rosado	Pink
Verde	Green

Table 6. Most commonly used colors in Spanish

By default, colors are masculine. But when they agree with a feminine subject, their spelling changes. For example, "vestido rosado" (pink dress) refers to a masculine noun (vestido). So, "rosado" is spelled with an "o" ending. In the case of a feminine noun, "camisa rosada" (pink shirt), "camisa" is considered feminine. As such, "rosada" now has an "a" ending in order to signal that it is feminine and not masculine.

The situation changes somewhat when you factor in singular and plural. So, "vestidos rosados" (pink dresses) agrees both in terms of gender and number. The "s" ending indicates that it is plural. In the case of "camisas rosadas," the same situation applies.

Notice also that both the adjective and noun must be singular or plural in order to maintain the proper agreement.

There are a couple of exceptions, though. Azul, gris, verde, and marrón do not change in terms of gender but do agree in terms of number. So, "botas grises" (grey boots), where "botas" is feminine plural, would be the same as "coches grises" (grey cars), where "coches" is masculine plural.

Please keep this in mind, as there are exceptions from time to time. Bear in mind that virtually all adjectives in Spanish have a singular and plural form, even if they are considered uncountable in English. For instance, "un pan" (a bread) may refer to individual units of bread in Spanish, where "bread" in uncountable in English.

Also, in Spanish, adjectives come after nouns. So, "cielo azul" (blue sky) is the opposite of the proper English syntax. Please keep this in mind so that you can avoid confusing your interlocutors when speaking.

Telling the Time

The next topic covered in this chapter is time.

Time is a rather straightforward topic in Spanish. However, there are a couple of differences.

For starters, time is generally based on a 24-hour clock rather than two, 12-hour clocks. So, the morning hours are expressed from "cero horas" (zero hours, or midnight) to "doce horas" (twelve hours, or midday). After midday, time is expressed as "trece horas" (thirteen hours), all the way up to "veinticuatro horas" or midnight. Once the new day begins, time is then reset to "zero hours." This distinction is made in order to avoid confusion between am and pm times.

For instance, if you have an appointment at 7 o'clock in the evening, you could express it at "diecinueve horas en punto" (nineteen hours "on point"). The expression, "on point" is used to indicate that it is the beginning of the hour or "o'clock" in English.

It is also possible to express time on a 12-hour basis. However, it is important to include the specific time of day you are referring to. So, "ten o'clock in the morning" would be "diez de la mañana." Afternoon hours would be referred to as "de la tarde." For instance, "cinco de la tarde" (17:00 or 5 pm) is referring to a time that is past midday.

Now, here is an interesting difference between English and Spanish. Spanish does not account for "evening." As a matter of fact, as soon as the sun goes down and it gets dark, the time then becomes "noche" or night. So, "seis de la tarde" would be "six in the afternoon" since the sun doesn't typically finish setting by this time. However, "siete de la noche" (seven at night) would be logical since it is normal for it to be dark around this time. So, the rule of thumb is that as soon as it is completely dark, you can begin to use "night."

This also applies to greetings, like "goodnight" or "buenas noches," which is the applicable greeting whenever it is completely dark. However, if there is still a twinge of sunlight, then it would still be proper to use "buenas tardes" (good afternoon).

Fractional portions of hours also have their own particular expressions.

- "cuarto" refers to "quarter." So, "es un cuarto después de las dos" (it's a quarter past two) refers to 2:15. "Un cuarto para las dos," (a quater to two) refers to 1:45. Please notice the difference in the use of "después" (after) and "para" (to) when referring to time.
- Also, the use of "media" (half) makes it clear that you are talking about half hours. So, "son las tres y media" (It is three and a half) is the same as saying "half past," or 30 minutes past the hour.

- Other fractional hours can be expressed using the exact number of minutes. So, "es la una y venticinco" (it's one twenty-five) refers to 1:25.
- Please notice that hours are always expressed in the plural form, except for one. Hours are feminine, but minutes are masculine. Nevertheless, your expression of time will always make reference to the feminine form and not the masculine form.

When in doubt, you can always refer to time by expressing the numbers themselves. For example, you can say, "son las cuatro y cinco" (it's four and five), that is, 4:05. You will not be questioned if you are referring to am or pm when giving the current time, but you might be asked to clarify if you are referring to a future time. So, be sure to use "de la mañana," "de la tarde," or "de la noche" in order to clarify the time of day you are referring to.

Now, let us move on to the days of the week.

- lunes (Monday)
- martes (Tuesday)
- miércoles (Wednesday)
- jueves (Thursday)
- viernes (Friday)
- sábado (Saturday)
- domingo (Sunday)

Please note that the days of the week are not capitalized in Spanish. In fact, they are written in lowercase letters. For example, "hoy es lunes" (Today is Monday) illustrates how the days of the week are not capitalized.

Also, here are the months of the year.

- enero (January)
- febrero (February)
- marzo (March)
- abril (April)
- mayo (May)
- junio (June)
- july (Julio)
- agosto (August)
- septiembre (September)
- octubre (October)
- noviembre (November)
- diciembre (December)

Just like the days of the week, months are not written with capitals. So, a formal date such as "lunes, tres de septiembre" (Monday, September third) would not be expressed in capitals. Also, please note that dates are written out in nominal number and not in ordinal numbers like in the case of English.

With regard to years, there is no split between the digits of a year. For example, the year "2010" would be "dos mil diez," that is, "two thousand ten." So, keep this in mind any time you are talking about a year.

Here are some examples:

- 1991 (mil novecientos noventa y uno – one thousand nine hundred and ninety-one)
- 2002 (dos mil dos – two thousand two)
- 1885 (mil ochocientos ochenta y cinco – one thousand eight hundred and eighty-five)

Keep this important difference in mind when talking about years.

Expressing Feelings

The last item in this chapter refers to feelings.

Generally speaking, feelings are adjectives, which agree in gender and number. This implies that you need to be aware if you are talking about yourself or others in the singular and/or plural form.

As such, a question such as "¿Cómo estás?" (how are you?) can be replied with:

- Estoy bien. (I am fine)
- Estoy cansado/a (I am tired)
- Estoy feliz (I am happy)

Notice how "feliz" does not have a gender agreement but would have a plural agreement as "feliz" (singular) and "felices" (happy in plural form).

Here is a list of the most common feelings in the Spanish language.

Spanish	English
Feliz	Happy
Enamorado/a	In love
Aburrido/a	Bored
Cansado/a	Tired
Asustado/a	Scared
Enojado/a	Angry
Celoso/a	Jealous
Sorprendido/a	Surprised
Content/a	Happy, satisfied
Nervioso/a	Nervous
Ocupado/a	Busy
Preocupado/a	Worried
Furioso/a	Furious
Triste	Sad
Avergonzado/a	Embarrassed
Optimista	Optimistic
Relajado/a	Relaxed
Fatal	Terrible, awful

Table 7. Most commonly used colors in Spanish

Notice how most of the adjectives are presented as "o/a" in order to indicate their masculine or feminine form. There are a couple of exceptions, such as "feliz," "triste," and "optimista," which do not have a specific gender form. So, please make sure to use them without changing their ending. Nevertheless, they do have a singular and plural form. So, make sure to keep this in mind.

In the next chapter, we will dig deeper into the use of adjectives, nouns, and articles and how you can use the vocabulary covered in this chapter in order to make sentences and express your ideas in a clear manner.

Chapter 9: Nouns, Articles, and Adjectives

Adjectives

In the previous chapter, we discussed colors and feelings. This was our introduction to adjectives. As such, adjectives work the same way in Spanish as they do in English. Adjectives are used to describe nouns and even other adjectives.

Any number of words can qualify as adjectives: numbers, feelings, colors, materials, size, and other general descriptors. One very important difference between English and Spanish is that adjectives don't necessarily have a specific order which they must follow. This means is that you can basically list adjectives in any way that you feel makes sense and is understandable to your interlocutors.

So, let's take a look at how each type of adjective can be used in a conversation:

- **Numbers**. Numbers used to indicate quantity can be used like any other type of adjective. For instance, "un dólar" (one dollar) or "veinte dólares" (twenty dollars) can be used in this manner. Notice that "uno dólar" is not used but "un" is. This is done only when the number "uno" is used as an adjective to indicate quantity. Numbers do not agree in gender or have singular/plural forms.
- **Feelings**. As indicated in the previous chapter, feelings must agree in terms of number and gender. Also, mind the exceptions.
- **Colors**. As indicated in the previous chapter, colors must agree in terms of number and gender. Also, mind the exceptions.
- **Materials**. Materials, that is, what objects are made of, are also common adjectives. For instance, "lana" (wool) "madera" (wood), "cuero" (leather), "vidrio" (glass), "plástico" (plastic), and "metal" (metal) are the most common materials you can find. These materials are not gender-specific and don't have singular/plural agreement. So, "sillas de madera" (wooden chairs) has its plural noun (sillas), but the adjective (madera) remains singular. The reason for this is that you are using the preposition "de" to indicate the material that it is made of. As such, you are literally saying "chairs of wood."
- **Size**. Words, such as "pequeño" (small), "mediano" (medium), and "grande" (large) are common adjectives used to refer to size. In this case, you need to agree in terms of gender and number. So, "sillas pequeñas" (small chairs) agrees both in terms of gender and number. In the case of "grande," it is gender-neutral but must agree in terms of number. Other size-related adjectives include "chiquito" (tiny), "enorme" (enormous), "largo" (long), "corto" (short), "ancho" (wide), and "angosto" (narrow), which you can use.
- **General descriptors**. In this group, we can find phrases such as "Bueno" (good), "malo" (bad), and expressions, such as "excelente" (excellent) and "terrible" (terrible, awful) to use to describe people, things, and situations in general terms.

Here is a list of adjectives referring to personal qualities and characteristics, which you will surely find useful when describing people.

- Alto/a = tall
- Bajo/a = short
- Flaco/a = skinny
- Delgado/a = thin
- Gordo/a = fat
- Rubio/a = blonde
- Moreno/a = dark
- Pelirrojo/a = redhead

Once again, you will notice that there is the need to ensure agreement in both terms of gender and number.

Articles

The next item to be covered in this chapter deals with articles. In Spanish, articles are related to both gender and number.

So, let's look at the articles related to gender.

In the singular form, the masculine singular article is "e l." Please note that the pronoun "él" refers to "he." In this case, the difference is the tilde on the "e." This serves no other purpose but to differentiate the article from the pronoun.

In the case of the feminine singular, the pronoun used is "la." For example, "la luna" (the moon) makes it clear that you are talking about the singular form of a feminine noun. By the same token, "el sol" (the sun) is masculine. As such, it is masculine and singular, hence the use of "el."

So, anytime you are referring to singular nouns, it is important to keep in mind that they will use either "el" or "la," depending on their gender. There are no gender-neutral nouns in Spanish. That is why it is important to keep in mind that even objects will have a gender assigned to them.

The general rule of thumb is to look out for the ending in their names. As such, nouns that end in "o" are typically masculine, while nouns ending in "a" are generally feminine. Of course, there are several exceptions. For example, "el agua" (water) is actually masculine, while "la radio" (radio) are exceptions to the rule.

The best piece of advice, in this case, is to make sure that you take note of the gender assigned to the various words you run into. That way, you can become familiar with both the general rules and the exceptions.

The plural articles play off the singular ones. So, "el" (masculine singular) will be "los" (masculine plural). For instance, "el coche" (the car) is a singular, masculine noun. "Los coches" (the cars) would be its plural form. In this manner, singular, masculine nouns will take the plural form they need.

With regard to feminine nouns, "la computadora" (the computer) will then become "las computadoras" in the plural, feminine form. Just like the masculine form, the article changes, along with the addition of the letter “s” at the end of it. This makes the agreement work perfectly as per Spanish orthographic rules.

To sum up, these are masculine and feminine articles:

- “el” (the, masculine, singular)
- “los” (the, masculine, singular)
- “la” (the, feminine, singular)
- “las” (the, feminine, singular)

Also, note that the indefinite article “a/an” in English is not used in Spanish. If you are referring to a singular object, you can use “un” (one) to refer to it.

Nouns

The third item in this chapter pertains to nouns.

In Spanish, nouns work in exactly the same way as they do in English. Nouns are a person, place, or thing. As such, there is not much guesswork in this regard.

On the whole, nouns can be classified as common nouns, proper nouns, abstract, concrete, individual, and collective.

Common nouns are those which refer to any person, place, or thing that is not the official name of it. For instance, “perro” (dog), “aire” (aire), and “lápiz” (pencil) are some examples of common nouns.

Proper nouns are the official names of people, countries, and titles. Names such as Juan, Pedro, María, and Teresa are just some examples. If a name is not typically Spanish and imported into Spanish, they must still be capitalized. The same goes for surnames, regardless of their origin. Names of countries are capitalized, but nationalities are not. So, “Alemania” (Germany) is capitalized as it is the name of a country, but “alemán” (German) is not capitalized as it refers to the nationality. Street names are also capitalized.

Other nouns which are not capitalized in Spanish are days of the week and months of the year. So, “lunes” (Monday) is not capitalized just as “marzo” (March) is not.

Here is a quick list of the days of the week:

- lunes (Monday)
- martes (Tuesday)
- miércoles (Wednesday)
- jueves (Thursday)
- viernes (Friday)
- sábado (Saturday)
- domingo (Sunday)

Here are the months of the year.

- enero (January)
- febrero (February)

- marzo (March)
- abril (April)
- mayo (May)
- junio (June)
- julio (July)
- agosto (August)
- septiembre (September)
- octubre (October)
- noviembre (November)
- diciembre (December)

As far as concrete and abstract nouns go, these are nouns which can either be physically perceived in some way or not. For example, "gato" (cat) is a concrete noun as it can be perceived and physically exists while "justiciar" (justice) is an idea which is considered a noun but does not have an actual, physical manifestation.

Collective and individual nouns are another term for singular and plural nouns. However, there are nouns which are considered to be individual and others which are considered to be collective. For instance, "mujer" (woman) is an individual noun as it represents one, individual woman. On the other hand, "flota" (fleet) refers to a group of ships. As such, it is collective. Now, you might see "la flota" (the fleet) and think it is singular, which is true, but it is collective nonetheless, as it is referring to a group of ships.

If you are ever in doubt about whether a noun is singular, plural, collective, and so on, the RAE online dictionary can help you determine the official form of a word. The RAE is the definitive party on this matter. So, feel free to consult it any time you are unsure or unclear about any terms in Spanish.

Chapter 10: Plurals

In Spanish, both nouns and adjectives are plurals. So, you need to make sure that both adjectives and nouns agree when you are constructing a sentence. While we have gone over some of the most important aspects of the plural form in previous chapters, we are now going to focus on the guidelines that come with building plurals in Spanish.

Word Ending in a Vowel

Nouns and adjectives that end in a vowel should have an "s" added to them. This is applicable to any noun or adjective that ends in a vowel, "a," "e," "i," "o," or "u." Some examples include:

- Silla (chair) – sillas (chairs)
- Teléfono (telephone) – teléfonos (telephones)
- Taxi (cab) – taxis (cabs)
- Buque (boat) – buques (boats)
- Tribu (tribe) – tribus (tribes)

The same goes for words that end in an accentuated vowel, that is, with a tilde at the end of it. For example:

- Bebé (baby) – Bebés (babies)
- Papá (father) – papás (fathers/parents)
- Buró (office) – burós (offices)

However, in the case of "ú" and "í," "es" is added to make the plural form. For instance:

- Tabú (taboo) – tabúes (taboos)
- Colibrí (hummingbird) – colibríes (hummingbirds)

In this case, it is more of a pronunciation device than an orthographic one. As such, please pay attention to the words ending in "í" and "ú." The good news is that words with these endings are quite as common as the first group.

Also, the "í" ending is applicable to some demonyms. For example:

- paquistaní (Pakistaní) – paquistaníes (Pakistanis)
- iraní (Iranian) – iraníes (Iranians)
- iraquí (Iraqi) – iraquíes (Iraqis)

While most demonyms generally end in "iego" or "és," the "í" tends to be a bit of a special case. For other demonyms, you will add the "es" ending:

- danés (Dane) – daneses (Danes)
- finlandés (Finn) – finlandéses (finns)
- irlandés (Irish) – irlandéses(Irish)

Also,

- griego (Greek) – griegos (Greeks)

All other demonyms would just have the "s" added to it.

Words Ending in Consonants

In the case of words that end in "y," the "es" ending is required to make the plural form. For instance:

- ley (law) – leyes (laws)
- rey (king) – reyes (kings)
- lady (Lady, as in noble rank) – ladys (Ladies)

While the "y" ending isn't all that common, you will certainly run into a few words containing this ending.

Also, please bear in mind that all words ending in "s" (in singular form) and "x" shall have the "es" ending added to it.

For example:

- fax (fax) – faxes (faxes)
- compás (compass) – compáses (compasses)

Given the nature of the "s" being the plural ending, there aren't many words that end in "s" in their singular form. The ones that do don't generally change. For example:

- el virus – los virus
- el viernes – los Viernes
- la crisis – las crisis
- el tórax – los tórax

The previous examples illustrate how these words remain the same in their singular and plural forms. In addition, words ending in "z" will have the "es" ending added but with the "z" changing to "c." For instance:

- pez (fish) – peces (fish)
- voz (voice) – voces (voices)
- feroz (fierce) – feroces (fierce)

Words that end in "l," "r," n," "d," and "j," so long as they follow a vowel, will also have the "es" ending added to it.

Some examples of this rule are as follows:

- barril (barrel) – barriles (barrels)
- amor (loves) – amores (loves)
- camión (truck) – camiones (trucks)
- actividad (activity) – actividades (activities)
- reloj (clock) – relojes (clocks)

In addition, words ending in any other consonant that isn't the ones we have listed above would simply have "s" added to it. This is mainly due to pronunciation more than any orthographic reason. Here are some examples:

- álbum – álbums (albums)
- bóxer – bóxers (boxers, sport)
- cómic – cómics (comics)
- póster – pósters (posters)
- superávit – superávits (surpluses)

These words do not take the "es" ending in the plural form. It should be noted that these words are not nearly as common as those that take the "es" ending. Another thing to keep in mind is that the majority of these terms have been originally imported from other languages. As such, they tend to maintain the same structure from their original languages.

Nouns With Two or More Words and Proper Nouns

In the event of nouns that are made up of two or more words, all of the words need to become plural. This maintains the overall singular/plural structure of that noun. Consider the following examples:

- Los Estados Unidos (The United States)
- Las Naciones Unidas (The United Nations)
- Estados miembros (member states)
- Sus Majestades (Their Majesties)
- Sus Altezas Reales (Their Royal Highness)
- Buenos Aires (the city of Buenos Aires)

The above examples are generally limited to formal titles or designations. Nevertheless, each word that makes up the whole noun is plural, as it is part of the whole name, title, or designation.

Also, when you are talking about a family, the surname is not pluralized. So, if you are to the Smith family, you would have "los Smith." By the same token, the Rodríguez family would be "los Rodríguez." As such, surnames are never pluralized.

This previous point also applies to brand names. This is true in the event that you are referring to various objects by the brand and not their actual name, for example, los coches Toyota (the Toyota cars). In this example, you wouldn't pluralize the brand name, as it is a proper noun just like names and surnames. Consequently, you can pluralize the noun itself (car, in this case) but without pluralizing the brand. Here are some more examples:

- Zapatillas Nike (Nike sneakers)
- Chocolates Snickers (Snickers chocolates)
- Computadoras Dell (Dell computers)
- Relojes Omega (Omega watches)
- Gafas de sol Ray-Ban (Ray-Ban sunglasses)

Even if you referred to the items as if their brand was a noun, it would still not be pluralized. Take the example, “los Ford son muy buenos” (Fords are very good). While you would pluralize the brand name in English, you wouldn’t do so in Spanish, especially if their brand name is originally from another language.

The same concept extends to the name of companies. When a company opens several branches or offices, such as in the case of banks, you won't use the company’s name in the plural form. You would only limit yourself to expressing the name of the company in relation to the number of offices opened. For example, “han abierto tres nuevos Walmart en la ciudad” (Three new Walmarts have been opened). The main reasoning behind this rule is that it is hard to determine what the proper plural form would be. So, it is much easier to keep the name as singular. In the event that you do hear people refer to companies and brands in the plural form, it might be due to colloquialisms from locals more than actual grammatical logic.

Chapter 11: Pronouns

In Spanish, pronouns have the same function as they do in English. The main function of a pronoun is to substitute a common or proper noun. In that regard, pronouns are used to take the place of nouns in the subject or object position.

Personal Pronouns

So, let's first dive into the pronouns in the subject position. This is where personal pronouns come into play. In Spanish, subject pronouns function in the same way as they do in English but do have a bit of a different structure.

- Yo (I)
- Tú (you informal, singular)
- Usted (you formal, singular)
- Él (he, singular)
- Ella (she, singular)
- Nosotros (we, plural)
- Ellos (they masculine, plural)
- Ellas (they feminine, plural)
- Ustedes (you, plural)

As you can see, the structure of subject pronouns is essentially the same in Spanish as they are in English. However, there are some differences. These differences are related to the very essence and nature of the language.

For starters, you will notice that there are two forms of "you." The first form; that is, "tú" is the informal version. This can be used among friends, family, peers, colleagues, and anyone with whom you are on a friendly basis. In most countries, it is not recommended to use this form when addressing strangers. As such, "tú" is used when you have some type of relationship with a person that is not based on a hierarchical context. For example, it is uncommon to use "tú" with your boss or superiors unless you are invited to do so.

It is quite common for men of the same age and rank to use this form among themselves. However, men should take care of not automatically using this form to address women, especially if they are in a formal business context.

So, if you find yourself in a formal context, "usted" is the best way to go. This form can be used to address strangers in public places and with people who are older or have a higher rank than you. For instance, if you are addressing public officials, these individuals have a higher rank and therefore, command respect even if it is simply a social convention.

A good example of this is the military. Officers of higher rank would address those of lower rank by using "tú." However, those soldiers of lower rank would have to address their superiors by using "usted" as a sign of respect for the rank and office they hold.

Another interesting difference is the lack of a gender-neutral pronoun. As such, "it" does not exist in Spanish since every single noun is assigned a gender. Consequently, all objects, including animals, must be referred to with its corresponding gender.

There is also the use of "ellos" and "ellas" in reference to "they." Given the fact that English does not assign gender, only one pronoun is necessary. In this case, please bear in mind that there is a clear distinction when referring to the gender of nouns in the plural form.

Also, the use of "ustedes" as the plural form of "you" makes a clear distinction for the singular and plural forms of "you." This is a significant difference with English as English does not contemplate a plural version of "you."

As you gain experience with Spanish, you may encounter the use of "vos" and "vosotros." These two forms are not widely used in Latin America. In fact, their use is limited to a handful of countries. "Vos" is the third form of "you," which is considered to be very informal. It marks the lowest level formality when addressing other folks. It is widely used in Argentina and Uruguay while used in Colombia but only when forming close relationships with people of similar age and rank. In Central America, the use of "vos" is rather co mmon, though it is only used when there is absolute confidence among people. It is seldomly used between men and women, though it is quite common among siblings.

"Vosotros" is the plural form of "vos." It is an informal way of referring to a group of people. However, it is basically used in Spain and considered archaic in Latin America. As such, you will hear this form used rather commonly in Spain but almost never in Latin America. In fact, if you were to use it in Latin America, you would get some funny looks from your interlocutors since it isn't all that common.

When referring to pronouns in the object position, that is, following the verb, the same batch of personal pronouns can be used in this context. For example, "Ella le habla a él" literally means "she speaks to he." In English, the proper form would be "She speaks to him." However, Spanish does not use a specific set of object pronouns in the same manner that English does. So, in a manner of speaking, it is a much simpler grammatical construct.

Possessive Pronouns

Next, we have possessive pronouns. These have the same function as they do in English. Let's take a look at these.

Personal	Possessive	English
Yo (I)	Mi	My
Tú (you informal, singular)	Tu	Your
Usted (you formal, singular)	Su	Your
Él (he, singular)	Su	His
Ella (she, singular)	Su	Her
Nosotros (we, plural)	Nuestro	Our
Ellos (they masculine, plural)	Su	Their
Ellas (they feminine, plural)	Su	Their
Ustedes (you, plural)	Su	Your

Table 8. Personal and possessive pronouns in Spanish

As you can see, the use of "su" can be used when referring to "usted," "él," and "ella," while "su" is also used as the plural form of these pronouns. Now, there are a couple of interesting differences.

Firstly, "tu," without a tilde, is the possessive pronoun form, whereas, "tú" with the tilde is "you." So, please be aware of this difference. While there is no difference in the pronunciation of either word, there is an orthographic function in this spelling difference.

Another key difference is that possessive pronouns are also subject to singular-plural agreement. So, if the object that agrees with the possessive pronoun (not the subject of the sentence) is plural, then the pronoun must also be plural. For instance, "Aquí están mis botas" (my boots are here), "mi" would be transformed into "mis." The same goes for "tu," as it becomes "tus" and "su" then changes to "tus." Also, "nuestro" becomes "nuestros." At the end of the day, all you need to do is add an "s" to make it plural.

Demonstrative Pronouns

Another batch of pronouns is known as "demonstrative pronouns." Here they are:

- Éste (this) – masculine
- Ésta (this) – feminine
- Éstos (these) – plural

- Ésa (that) – feminine
- Ése (that) – masculine
- Ésos (those) – plural
- Aquél (that) – masculine
- Aquélla (that) – feminine
- Aquéllos (those) – masculine plural
- Aquéllas (those) – feminine plural

Notice how these pronouns are equivalent to "this," "that," "these," and "those," though they do make a difference in terms of gender and number. Now, the basic difference between "ése" and "aquél" is the relative distance between the object and the speaker. For example, an object that is just beyond the speaker's reach would be "ése," while an object that is much farther away would be deemed as "aquél."

Also, please note that "ése," "ésa," "éste," and "ésta" are considered inappropriate for people. As such, they can be considered to be rude. So, when referring to a person, it is better to use "aquél" or "aquélla." Nevertheless, out of politeness, it is best to use a person's name or title rather than a pronoun.

You might hear "ése," for instance, used to refer to people. However, this pronoun is used either in a very informal context or even in a derogatory tone. So, please be on the lookout for such usage.

On the whole, you will find that the use of pronouns in Spanish is very similar to English. While there are some differences in terms of gender and number, the underlying concept is the same. So, do take the time to go over them and become familiar with their use in conversation.

Chapter 12: Verbs

Regular Verbs

In this chapter, we are going to focus on the use of verbs in the present simple tense. As such, we are going to be looking at verb conjugations and the patterns that come with the various types of verbs.

First, the key to conjugation Spanish verbs is based on the end of the verb in its infinitive form. It should be noted that the infinitive form means that the verb does not have a tense, i.e., past, present, or future.

There are three endings to all Spanish verbs in their infinitive form: AR, ER, and IR.

As such, all Spanish verbs will have one of these endings. Here are some examples:

- ER ending
    - Comer (to eat)
    - Conocer (to know)
    - Entender (to understand)
    - Volver (to return)
    - Responder (to respond)
- IR ending
    - Vivir (to live)
    - Sentir (to feel)
    - Permitir (to permit)
    - Confundir (to confuse)
    - Exigir (to demand)
- AR ending
    - Cargar (to load)
    - Hablar (to speak)
    - Arreglar (to arrange)
    - Jugar (to play)
    - Andar (to go)

The conjugation for these verbs follows a similar pattern, though there is a slight variation based on the ending. These variations are due more to pronunciation issues rather than grammatical concerns. Nevertheless, you will see that they are very similar and should soon become second nature to you as you gain more practice and experience.

Let us see the conjugation patterns for the ER-ending verbs below.

- Verb: Comer (to eat)
    - Yo com**o** (I eat)
    - Tú com**es** (you eat)
    - Usted com**e** (you eat)
    - Él com**e** (he eats)

    - Ella com**e** (they eat)
    - Nosotros com**emos** (we eat)
    - Ellos com**en** (they eat)
    - Ellas com**en** (they eat)
    - Usteded com**en** (you eat)

As you can see, the ER ending is dropped in favor of the proper ending based on the subject pronoun in question. In the case of "yo," an "o" is added. So, that basically means that you only drop the "r" from the ending of the verb and switch the "e" for an "o." In the case of "tú," an "es" is added. As for you "usted," "él," and "ella," an "e" is added to the ending. "Nosotros" requires the addition of "emos," while "ellos," "ellas," and "ustedes" get the "en" ending.

That's basically it. The rest of the verbs will have some variations to them. Nevertheless, the basic pattern is the same.

Let's have a look at the verbs ending in IR:

- Verb: vivir (to live)
    - Yo viv**o** (I live)
    - Tú viv**es** (you live)
    - Usted viv**e** (you live)
    - Él viv**e** (he lives)
    - Ella viv**e** (he lives)
    - Nosotros viv**imos** (we live)
    - Ellos viv**en** (they live)
    - Ellas viv**en**(they live)
    - Ustedes viv**en** (you live)

As you can see, the pattern is the same as the exception in the conjugation of "nosotros." In this case, the "emos" ending is modified slightly to "imos." Aside from that, the rest of the endings are exactly the same.

Now, let's take a look at the AR endings:

- Verb: hablar (to speak)
    - Yo habl**o** (I speak)
    - Tú habl**as** (you speak)
    - Usted habl**a** (you speak)
    - Él habl**a** (he speaks)
    - Ella habl**a** (she speaks)
    - Nosotros habl**amos** (we speak)
    - Ellos habl**an** (they speak)
    - Ellas habl**an** (they speak)
    - Ustedes habl**an** (you speak)

With this verb ending, there are slight differences. First, with the "tú" conjugation, the verb changes from "es" to "as." Also, in the "nosotros" conjugation, the verb ending changes from "emos" or "imos" to "amos." Also, the "en" endings are changed to "an." These changes are due to the fact that the verb ends in AR. Hence, the endings reflect the change in pronunciation, as opposed to a specific grammar rule. Nevertheless, the pattern remains the same. As such, you can easily get into the mechanics of conjugating these verbs.

Irregular Verbs

The conjugation patterns mentioned above are related to regular verbs. That means that there is a list of irregular verbs which you need to become familiar with. While this list is rather small, it contains some of the most common verbs you will use in conversation.

Let's take a look at the list:

- Dar (to give)
- Decir (to say)
- Estar (to be)
- Hacer (to do)
- Ir (to go)
- Oir (to hear)
- Pedir (to ask)
- Poder (can)
- Poner (to put)
- Querer (to want)
- Saber (to know)
- Seguir (to follow)
- Ser (to be)
- Tener (to have)
- Venir (to come)
- Ver (to see)

As you can see, all of these verbs maintain the AR, ER, and IR structure in their infinitive form. However, their structure makes it rather difficult to follow the same pattern that regular verbs follow. So, let's take a look at how these verbs are conjugated.

Person	dar	decir	estar	hacer	ir	oir	pedir	poder
Yo	doy	digo	estoy	hago	voy	oigo	pido	puedo
Tú	das	dices	estás	haces	vas	oyes	pides	puedes
Usted	da	dice	está	hace	va	oye	pide	puede
Él	da	dice	está	hace	va	oye	pide	puede
Ella	da	dice	está	hace	va	oye	pide	puede
Nosotros	damos	decimos	estamos	hacemos	vamos	oímos	pedimos	podemos
Ellos	dan	dicen	están	hacen	van	oyen	piden	pueden

Ellas	dan	dicen	están	hacen	van	oyen	piden	pueden
Ustedes	dan	dicen	están	hacen	van	oyen	piden	pueden

Person	**poner**	**querer**	**saber**	**seguir**	**ser**	**tener**	**venir**	**ver**
Yo	pongo	quiero	sé	sigo	soy	tengo	vengo	veo
Tú	pones	quieres	sabes	segues	eres	tienes	vienes	ves
Usted	pone	quiere	sabe	sigue	es	tiene	viene	ve
Él	pone	quiere	sabe	sigue	es	tiene	viene	ve
Ella	pone	quiere	sabe	sigue	es	tiene	viene	ve
Nosotros	ponemos	queremos	sabemos	seguimos	somos	temenos	venimos	vemos
Ellos	ponen	quieren	saben	siguen	son	tienen	vienen	ven
Ellas	ponen	quieren	saben	siguen	son	tienen	vienen	ven
Ustedes	ponen	quieren	saben	siguen	son	tienen	vienen	ven

Table 9. Irregular verbs in Spanish conjugated in the present simple.

The list above is intended to serve as a reference. As such, you will be able to use this table when you are going through verb lists and exercises. Please note that the structure does not vary significantly with each verb. Nevertheless, they do vary enough, so you need to pay attention to the way each of the verbs is written out.

Another note is if you are unsure whether a verb is irregular, you can assumethat it is regular. The chances of a verb being irregular are far less than being regular. That is why the best piece of advice you can take into consideration at this point is that practice makes perfect. As you gain more practice and experience with verbs, you will easily recognize the patterns among regular and irregular verbs, so the amount of trouble you will have while figuring your conjugations will be far less than you had imagined initially.

Chapter 13: Ser and Estar

"Ser" and "estar" are the two most important verbs in the Spanish language. They serve as both verbs and auxiliaries within the various tenses. That is why we have devoted an entire chapter to discussing both verbs.

First of all, both "ser" and "estar" translate into "to be" in English. What this means is that if you look them up, they will both be reflected as "to be." So, what's the difference?

There are two main differences between each one. The first is that "ser" refers to things that are considered permanent or that are unlikely to change. This applies to personal information, such as your name, address, nationality, and so on. While any of these bits of information could potentially change, it is highly unlikely that they will.

"Estar" refers to states, which by definition, are considered less permanent. Feelings are a prime example. Since your feelings are much more likely to change, "estar" would be the verb of choice. "Estar" does have one other important function; it is used as an auxiliary verb, especially when constructing continuous tenses. As such, you can use it in combination with the main verb of the sentence in order to produce the tense you wish to use.

Ser – "to be"

So, let's begin by looking at the conjugation of "ser."

- Yo soy (I am)
- Tú eres (you are)
- Usted es (you are)
- Él es (he is)
- Ella es (she is)
- Nosotros somos (we are)
- Ellos son (they are)
- Ellas son (they are)
- Ustedes son (you are)

With this in mind, you can express ideas such as the following:

- Yo soy de Alemania. (I am from Germany)
- Tú eres un turista. (You are a tourist)
- Usted es mi amiga. (You are my friend)
- Él es amigable. (He is friendly)
- Ella es interesante. (She is interesting)
- Nosotros somos nuevos estudiantes. (We are new students)
- Ellos son los mejores trabajadores. (They are the best workers)
- Ellas son mis hermanas. (They are my sisters)
- Ustedes son especiales. (You are special)

In all of these examples, we can see how we are either making a general description or stating a fact about this person. Granted, saying something like, "Él es amigable" isn't exactly a fact but an opinion. Nevertheless, we are stating a personal characteristic or trait about this person. As such, we would use the "ser" version of "to be."

Also, note that in case where you are referring to a plural subject, adjectives and nouns must agree with that subject. Hence, "ellas son mis hermanas" means that "mis" and "hermanas" need to be in the plural form in order to make sense of the subject which you are utilizing.

Estar — "to be"

Now, in the case of "estar," things shift from discussing permanent states to more changeable ones. For instance, feelings, current arrangements, and other changing circumstances are expressed by using "estar."

So, let's have a look at the conjugation of this verb:

- Yo estoy (I am)
- Tú estás (you are)
- Usted está (you are)
- Él está (he is)
- Ella está (she is)
- Nosotros estamos (we are)
- Ellos están (they are)
- Ellas están (they are)
- Ustedes están (you are)

In this case, you can see that the English version of this verb is exactly the same, though there is a clear difference in the Spanish conjugation. As such, you need to keep an eye out when using "estar," as opposed to "ser."

Consequently, you can make sentences such as the following:

- Yo estoy cansada. (I am tired)
- Tú estás aquí. (You are here)
- Usted está confundido. (You are confused)
- Él está en casa. (He is at home)
- Ella está enferma. (She is sick)
- Nosotros estamos en camino. (We are on the way)
- Ellos están locos. (They are crazy)
- Ellas están seguras. (They are sure)
- Ustedes están en lo correcto. (You are right)

As you can see, the above examples with the "estar" verb refer to feelings, location, and other states. You can use this verb to indicate more about the subject of the sentence, be it a person or an object.

The other important use of "estar" lies with the present continuous. In Spanish, the present continuous has the same function as in English; that is, to talk about actions that are happening at the time of speaking or temporary actions that are taking place around the present time.

Consequently, "estar" is used as an auxiliary, while the main verb of the sentence is transformed from its infinitive form to the "ando" or "iendo" form. The good news is that there is only one conjugation for the main verb since the agreement with the subject takes place with the verb "estar" and not the main verb.

Consider this example:

- Nosotros estamos estudiando inglés. (We are studying English)

In this example, notice how "estudiar" (study) is transformed from its infinitive form to the present participle form "estudiando." When placed together with the "estar" form of the verb, the present continuous is formed.

It should be noted that the present continuous form is used to talk about future actions in English. This function is not used in Spanish. So, please keep in mind that the present continuous in Spanish is limited to the present only.

Now, take note of how the present participle is conjugated through these examples:

- In the case of AR-ending verbs, add "ando" to the verb's ending. For example:
    - Jugar (to play) – jugando (playing)
    - Ahorrar (to save) – ahorrando (saving)
    - Hablar (to speak) – hablando (speaking)
    - Amar (to love) – amando (loving)
    - Gustar (to like) – gustando (liking)
- In the case of IR-ending verbs, add "iendo" to the verb's ending. For example:
    - Vivir (to live) – viviendo (living)
    - Mentir (to lie) – mintiendo (lying)
    - Sentir (to feel) – sintiendo (feeling)
    - Abolir (to abolish) – aboliendo (abolishing)
    - Abrir (to open) – abriendo (opening)
- In the case of ER-ending verbs, add "iendo" to the verb's ending. For example:
    - Correr (to run) – corriendo (running)
    - Comer (to eat) – comiendo (eating)
    - Hacer (to do) haciendo (doing)
    - Entender (to understand) – entendiendo (understanding)
    - Querer (to want) queriendo (wanting)

At this point, let's take a look at some real-life examples:

- Yo estoy viajando a Europa. (I am traveling to Europe)
- Tú estás viendo televisión. (You are watching television)
- Usted está hablando por teléfono. (You are speaking on the telephone)
- Él está jugando basquetbol. (He is playing basketball)
- Ella está escuchando música. (She is listening to music)

- Nosotros estamos comiendo en un restaurante. (We are eating at a restaurant)
- Ellos están estudiando matemáticas. (They are studying mathematics)
- Ellas están durmiendo en el coche. (They are sleeping in the car)
- Ustedes están comprando ropa. (You are buying clothes)

These examples all illustrate how the present continuous can be structured in order to talk about actions that are happening right at the time of speaking. However, the present continuous can also be used to talk about temporary actions.

Consider these examples:

- Yo estoy trabajando en una oficina. (I am working at an office)
- Él está viviendo en un departamento. (he is living in an apartment)
- Nosotros estamos estudiando inglés. (we are studying English)

Each of the previous examples serves to indicate that the action being discussed is temporary. As such, if the action described was meant to indicate a more permanent condition, then the present simple would be used. For instance:

- Yo trabajo en una oficina. (I work at an office)
- Él vive en un departamento. (he lives in an apartment)
- Nosotros estudiamos inglés. (we study English)

Consequently, the use of the present simple makes it clear that this is a situation that is unlikely to change any time soon. Therefore, using both tenses makes a clear distinction as to what you are trying to convey to your interlocutor.

At this point, it is worth mentioning how important getting a firm grasp of the "ser" and "estar" verbs really is. By gaining a good understanding of their functioning, you will be able to construct useful sentences and even begin to play around with the language in such a way that you can transmit the information that you want to get across in an accurate manner. So, it certainly pays to take the time to master these two essential verbs.

Chapter 14: Question Formation

In the Spanish language, there are two main types of questions: open-ended questions and yes or no questions.

The expected answer is "yes" or "no" to a typical yes or no question, and this is probably a part of any language. Of course, the answer can be expanded beyond the simple "yes" or "no." Nevertheless, the end result is a short answer.

Yes-or-No Questions

In order to form a question of this nature, you can take a regular statement and flip the subject and verb from their regular positions. Consider this example:

- Él viaja a Europa cada verano. (He travels to Europe every summer)

This is a regular statement in the affirmative. Now, to change it into a yes/no question, we need to switch the subject and verb so that they can reflect the change in syntax. Here is the new word order used to reflect the question.

- ¿Viaja él a Europa cada verano? (Does he travel to Europe every summer??

First of all, notice how the subject "él" moves from the first spot to the second, and the verb from the second to the first. This change enables the formation of a yes/no question.

Now, the answer to this question can be constructed as follows:

- ¿Viaja él a Europa cada verano? (Does he travel to Europe every summer?)
    - Sí, él viaja. (Yes, he travels.)
    - No, él no viaja. (No, he doesn't travel.)

Please notice that the negative form is constructed by the use of "no." So, you can see that there is no other auxiliary used in Spanish to make the negative form. All you need is to use "no" in order to transform the sentence from positive to negative.

The answers presented above are short answers. Of course, you can elaborate on these responses as much as you like. Nevertheless, you could reply something like:

- Sí, él viaja a Europa cada verano. (Yes, he travels to Europe every summer.)
- No, él no viaja a Europa cada verano. (No, he doesn't travel to Europe every summer.)

These longer-form answers can be used to make a point or simply elaborate further on the question being asked. It is not a requisite for you to express your answers in this manner, though it is an option that you have at your disposal.

Below are more examples of questions in Spanish.

- Yo como frutas todos los días. – ¿Como yo frutas todos los días?
- *I eat fruit every day. – Do I eat fruit every day?*
- Tú juegas fútbol cada viernes. – ¿Juegas tú fútbol cada viernes?

- *You play soccer every Friday. – Do you play soccer every Friday?*
- Usted vende ropa en una tienda – ¿Vende usted ropa en una tienda?
- *You sell clothes in a shop. – Do you sell clothes in a shop?*
- Él vive en Chicago. – ¿Vive él en Chicago?
- *He lives in Chicago. – Does he live in Chicago?*
- Ella trabaja en una oficina – ¿Trabaja ella en una oficina?
- *She works in an office. – Does she work in an office?*
- Nosotros bebemos refrescos en la cena. – ¿Bebemos nosotros refrescos en la cena?
- *We drink soda at dinner. – Do we drink soda at dinner?*
- Ellos hacen ejercicio en el gimnasio. – ¿Hacen ellos ejercicio en el gimnasio?
- *They do exercise at the gym. – Do they exercise at the gym?*
- Ellas cocinan pasteles los fines de semana. – ¿Cocinan ellas pasteles los fines de semana?
- *They bake cakes on the weekend. – Do they bake cakes on the weekend?*
- Ustedes escuchan música en el coche. – ¿Escuchan ustedes música en el coche?
- *You listen to music in the car. – Do you listen to music in the car?*

One of the most interesting characteristics of Spanish is that you can omit the subject of the sentence only when it is clear what you are talking about or to whom you are referring. This comes in very handy when asking questions as it is very common for native Spanish speakers to drop the subject, especially when they are addressing you directly.

Let us have a look at the previous examples without the use of the subject in the sentence.

- ¿Trabajas en una oficina? (Do you work in an office?)
  - Sí, trabajo en una oficina. (Yes, I work in an office.)
  - No, no trabajo en una oficina. (No, I don't work in an office.)

As you can see in this example, it is not needed to say, "¿Trabajas tú en una oficina?" It is enough to say, "¿Trabajas en una oficina?" since it is clear that the question is being addressed to "you" and not to anyone else.

Now, it should be noted that when you omit the subject of a sentence or question, it is important to be clear about whom you are referring to. Otherwise, this could lead to confusion and cause your interlocutor to seek clarification. So, it pays to be extra careful in order to avoid any potential confusion.

Open-Ended Questions

From yes/no questions, we can move on to open-ended questions. These types of questions allow for any type of response and not just a limited yes/no reply. As such, we need to use the set of questions words available.

Here are the questions words used in Spanish:

- Qué (what)

- Quién (who)
- Cuál (which)
- Cuándo (when)
- Cuánto (how much/many)
- Cómo (how)
- Dónde (where)
- Por qué (why)

Please note that question words have a tilde attached to them in order to differentiate them from the relative pronouns. For instance, "cuando" is not the same as "cuándo." While their spelling and pronunciation are identical, the tilde differentiates their function in writing.

Consider this example:

- Compro pan y leche cuando voy al supermercado. (I buy bread and milk when I go to the supermarket.)

In this example, we are using "cuando" as a relative pronoun since it is joining two separate parts of a sentence. Also, we omitted the use of "yo" since the sentence makes absolutely clear that I am referring to myself and no oneelse.

The use of "cuándo" in a question would work out like this:

- ¿Cuándo compras pan? (When do you buy bread?)

In this case, we need to carry the tilde on "cuándo" so that it is absolutely clear that we are talking about a question. While the structure and the context don't really leave much room for doubt, it is, nevertheless, important to make the point to avoid potential confusion.

Let's look at some more sample questions:

- ¿Dónde es mi lugar? (Where is my place?)
- ¿Cuándo vas a la escuela? (When do you go to school?
- ¿Cuántos años tiene? (How old are you?)
- ¿Quién es él? (Who is he?)
- ¿Qué bebe ella? (What does she drink?)
- ¿Por qué viajamos? (Why do we travel?)
- ¿Por qué trabajan ellos? (Why do they work?)
- ¿Cuál es la casa de ellas? (Which is their house?)
- ¿Cómo van al trabajo? (How do you get to work?)

There could be any number of responses to these questions. That is why they are open-ended. As such, it is up to you to find the right information that you would like to get across. For example:

- ¿Cuándo vas a la escuela? (When do you go to school?)
    - Voy a la escuela todos los días. (I go to school every day.)
    - Voy a la escuela en las noches. (I go to school at night.)
    - Voy a la escuela los fines de semana. (I go to school on weekends.)

- No voy a la escuela. (I don't go to school.)

As you can see, the potential responses can vary according to the information you are looking to provide your interlocutors.

Let us examine some common questions that you will come across when speaking Spanish.

- ¿Cuál es tu nombre? (What is your name?)
- ¿De dónde eres? (Where are you from?)
- ¿Dónde vives? (Where do you live?)
- ¿Cuántos años tienes? (How old are you?)
- ¿Cuál es tu número de teléfono? (What is your telephone number?)
- ¿Dónde trabajas? (Where do you work?)
- ¿Cuál es tu correo electrónico? (What is your email?)
- ¿Cuál es tu trabajo? (What do you do?)
- ¿Dónde queda el banco? (Where is the bank?)
- ¿Dónde está el baño? (Where is the bathroom?)

These are the most common questions that you will encounter when you are speaking to other folks. As such, these questions can come through for you in a pinch. So, do take the time to go over them, and put them into practice as often as you need to.

On the whole, question formation is a matter of practice. The more practice you are able to get structuring questions, the better you will become at asking the right questions when you need to. Best of all, Spanish syntax is flexible enough to where you could mix up the word order and still get the message across.

Consequently, you can make the most of your opportunity to travel without having to hesitate about getting directions or interacting with other folks. As you gain more proficiency, you will be able to construct your own scenarios based on your specific needs. That is why this guide will come in handy when you need a reference point.

Chapter 15: Adverbs, Prepositions, and Conjunctions

Adverbs

Adverbs have the same essential function in Spanish as they do in English. Basically, adverbs are used to describe verbs, adjectives, and other adverbs. This is what makes them a rather versatile part of speech. In short, the use of adverbs in Spanish is all about providing additional information that gives the sentence greater clarity.

First, we are going to take a closer look at the adverbs of time. These adverbs clarify information regarding time, when something takes place and the frequency with which it takes place. Consider the following adverbs:

- A menudo (often)
- Ahora (now)
- Algunas veces (sometimes)
- Anteriormente (previously)
- Antes (before)
- Ayer (yesterday)
- Después (after)
- Finalmente (lastly)
- Frecuentemente (frequently)
- Hoy (today)
- Luego (then)
- Mañana (tomorrow)
- Nunca (never)
- Ocasionalmente (occasionally)
- Posteriormente (afterward)
- Primeramente (firstly)
- Rara vez (rarely)
- Siempre (always)
- Ultimamente (lately)
- Ya (already)

These adverbs provide information about the time and frequency in which action happens. So, you can use them any time you wish to provide further clarification on the matter you are discussing. Consider these examples:

- Siempre estudiamos inglés por la mañana. (We always study English in the morning.)
- Los niños juegan ocasionalmente. (The children occasionally play.)
- Ellas van al cine mañana. (They go to the movies tomorrow.)
- Estoy en una reunión ahora. (I am in a meeting now.)
- Vamos a comer después del trabajo. (We are going to eat after work.)

Please note that the position of adverbs changes in these examples. In general, adverbs of time will go at the beginning of the sentence when the subject is omitted, as in "Siempre estudiamos inglés por la mañana." In this case, "siempre" goes at the beginning.

When the subject is included, the adverb tends to occupy the end of the expression unless it is part of an adverbial phrase, such as "después del trabajo." In this situation, the adverbial phrase acts as one, long adverb.

There is also one other possibility: you could place the adverb or adverbial phrase at the beginning of the sentence, followed by a comma. For example: "Hoy por la mañana, temenos una reunion." (This morning, we have a meeting.) In this example, we can see how the adverbial phrase is placed at the beginning of the sentence in order to establish time.

Given the fact that the previous examples illustrate the way adverbs are placed in a sentence, we can list other adverbs based on their categorization.

Place	Manner	Number	Affirmation	Negation	Doubt
Aquí	Así	Mucho	Sí	No	Quizá
Ahí	Bien	Poco	Claro	Tampoco	Tal vez
Acá	Mal	Más	Bueno	Nada	Acaso
Cerca	Major	Menos	Por supuesto	Apenas	Posiblemente
Lejos	Peor	Bastante	Naturalmente	Jamás	Seguramente
En frente	Como	Nada	Obviamente	Nunca	Probablemente
Debajo	Cuidadosamente	Cuanto	Definitivamente	Ninguno	Potencialmente
A la par	exitosamente	tanto	también	Para nada	Específicamente

Table 10. Adverbs in Spanish

Based on this list, you can gain or provide as much information as you need in order to get the message across. Considering that the location of adverbs is fairly straightforward, you can begin to construct your own sentences quickly and effectively.

Prepositions

With regard to prepositions, you can use them in basically the exact same manner as you would in English. In Spanish, prepositions are intended to indicate the relationship among elements in a sentence. Without them, sentences would lack consistency and logic. As such, the use of prepositions becomes critical when constructing logical sentences.

Spanish prepositions also have clear uses; that is, you can clearly determine in which cases a preposition is to be used.

The following chart illustrates the various propositions used in the Spanish language.

Spanish	English	Definition	Examples
A	TO/AT	Used to indicate direction, time, direction, frequency, object, manner, imperative	Vamos **a** tu casa. Tenemos reunion **a las** 10. Estudiamos inglés **a diario**. ¡**A** comer!
ANTE	BEFORE/ABOVE	Used to indicate location, preference	Todos somos iguales **ante** la ley. **Ante** todo, me gusta la pizza.
BAJO	UNDER	Used to indicate location and manner	La hoja está bajo el libro. No puedo trabajar **bajo** estas circunstancias.
CON	WITH	Used to indicate accompaniment, manner	Juego fútbol **con** mis amigos. Prepara la comida **con** cuidado.
DE	OF/FROM	Used to indicate origin and belonging	Soy **de** los Estados Unidos. Éste es el control **de** la televisión.
DESDE	SINCE/FROM	Used to indicate time and location.	Estudio inglés **desde** hace tres años. Trabajo **desde** mi casa.
DURANTE	DURING/FOR	Used to indicate the duration of time	Él habla **durante** horas.
EN	IN	Used to indicate the physical location, manner, and time.	El dinero está **en** el banco. No hacemos esto **en** mucho tiempo. Terminamos el reporte **en** 5 minutos.
ENTRE	AMONG	Used to indicate location	Estamos **entre** amigos.
EXCEPTO	EXCEPT	Used to indicate exclusion	Todos van **excepto** yo.
HACIA	TOWARD	Used to indicate direction	Vamos **hacia** la oficina.

HASTA	UNTIL	Used to indicate duration	Trabajamos **hasta** la media noche.
MEDIANTE	BY	Used to indicate manner	Nos pagan **mediante** cheque.
PARA	FOR	Used to indicate reason	Esto es **para** ella.
POR	BY	Used to indicate direction, objective and time	Jugamos **por** mucho tiempo. Caminamos **por** la calle. Ellos trabajan **por** dinero.
SEGÚN	ACCORDING TO	Used to indicate manner	**Según** mi jefe, hoy es día libre.
SIN	WITHOUT	Used to indicate exclusion	No puedo ir **sin** mi teléfono.
SOBRE	ABOUT/ON	Used to indicate location, topic	El dinero está **sobre** la mesa. Estamos hablando **sobre** temas importantes.

Table 11. Prepositions in Spanish

The previous chart is rather comprehensive and provides you with a solid overview of the preposition structure in Spanish. So, it certainly pays to become familiar with the various types of prepositions and their use. It should be noted that they don't always translate directly from English to Spanish and vice-versa. Nevertheless, the chart above makes a great effort to simplify this understanding. That way, you won't have to guess the right meaning for each preposition. Instead, you will be able to make consistent sentences every time.

Conjunctions

Conjunctions function in a similar manner as prepositions. They join two parts of a sentence together as long as they have consistency and logic. This allows the speaker, or writer, to express a more complex idea in a single statement. Consequently, conjunctions act as a connector between two or perhaps more ideas.

The three conjunctions we will discuss are "pero" (but), "y" (and), and "o" (or).

"Y" (and) is used to indicate inclusion; that is, it is used to join two ideas together. For example, "me gusta comer pizza y beber refrescos" (I like to eat pizza and drink sodas). In this example, we are joining two ideas that are related to each other. This has logic and consistency since the sentence flows naturally.

Also, "y" can be used in a list of items. For instance, "necesitamos comprar pan, leche, huevos y cereal." (We need to buy bread, milk, eggs, and cereal.) Notice that we use "y" at the end of the list. As such, you can join both ideas and items by using "y."

A word of caution: It is common to see the liberal use of "y" in writing. This is actually an improper form as it creates run-on sentences. While it is not in line with writing best practices in Spanish, it is commonly done.

Consider this example:

- Vamos de vacaciones a Europa y vamos a visitar muchos lugares y luego vamos a comer comida deliciosa y queremos conocer lugares nuevos y es una experiencia bonita" (We are going on vacation to Europe, and we are going to visit many places, and then we are going to eat Delicious food and then we are going to know new places, and it is a great experience.)

To English speakers, the problem with this sentence is rather obvious. However, it is not quite the same with Spanish speakers. So, be on the lookout for this type of writing. The best way to go in this case is to write shorter sentences. Something like this would sound a lot clearer and organized:

- Vamos de vacacione a Europa. Vamos a visitar muchos lugares. Luego, vamos a comer comida deliciosa. Queremos conocer lugares nuevos. Es una experiencia bonita.

This organization is much easier to follow and understand as opposed to the first example we presented.

The next preposition is "pero" (but). This preposition indicates contrast. By "contrast," we mean a different idea or opinion of consideration. This conjunction helps maintain consistency, as it reflects logical ideas in a proper context.

Consider this example: "me gusta la pizza pero no me gustan los refrescos." (I like pizza, but I don't like sodas.)

In this example, the contrast occurs when you have a food you like, followed by one which you don't. These contrasting ideas warrant the use of "pero." Your sentences can be as simple or complex as need be. Maintaining consistency is a skill you need to accomplish. Otherwise, your sentence can get confusing.

Take another example: "me gusta la pizza y me gustan los refrescos, pero no me gustan las hamburguesas." (I like pizza, and I like sodas, but I don't like hamburgers.) In this example, you have introduced two conjunctions in the same sentence. You could tighten up this idea by saying, "me gusta la pizza y los refrescos, pero no las hamburguesas." (I like pizza and sodas but not hamburgers.) This second version will help make your writing much easier to follow.

The last conjunction is "o" (or). It is used to indicate an alternative. In this case, alternatives serve as choices or options that are presented. It is important to note that there could be more than two options, though you would have to structure your ideas accordingly.

For example:

- Podemos comer pizza o hamburguesas. (We can eat pizza or hamburgers.)
- Podemos comer pizza, hamburguesas o pollo frito. (We can eat pizza, hamburgers, or fried chicken.)

In the first example, there are two options. In the second, there are three. As such, you could have an infinite number of options, but only the last one presented ought to be preceded by the "o" conjunction. Actually, "o" works in much the same way that "y" does in a list of items.

One interesting orthographic rule is when "o" is used to separate numbers, it carries a tilde. For instance: "¿Es el número 50 ó 15? (Is the number 50 or 15?)

The reason for using a tilde is to avoid potential confusion between "o" and "0." While the RAE has indicated that this rule is no longer mandatory, it is still widely used, especially in older texts, to avoid potential confusion between the conjunction and any numbers.

If you are going to present phrases as alternatives, ensure that you keep the same consistency throughout your writing.

For example: "podemos ir al cine o podemos ir a comer." (We can go to the movies, or we can go eat.)

While it would also be valid to say, "podermos ir al cine or a comer." (We can go to the movies or eat.), the use of "podemos" (we can) makes a case for its inclusion in the second half of the sentence in order to maintain consistency.

Granted, many of these ideas and structures are applicable to writing; it should be noted that when having a conversation, you can get away with not following these structures, as long as you are able to get your idea across. Nevertheless, it pays to follow the proper structure so that you can avoid confusing your interlocutors.

Just like any other part of speech or grammar practice is the best way for you to hone your skills. So, do take the time to go over any of the items in this chapter in order for you to make the most of the materials presented. In the next chapters, we are going to be putting this knowledge to the test. Therefore, be ready to put your thinking cap on and create some interesting sentences so that you can express your ideas.

Chapter 16: Forming Sentences

Sentence formation in Spanish is quite similar to that in English. Spanish and English syntax are very similar despite several differences. We have spoken about these differences throughout this book. However, we are going to put them all together in this chapter.

First of all, the basic structure of a Spanish sentence is based on the "subject + verb + object" formula. This means that you can take this basic structure to build any sentence that you would like to construct. Let's see how we can build a sentence in the present simple.

- Yo juego fútbol todos los días. (I play soccer every day).

In this example, the subject is "yo" (I), the verb is "juego" (play, conjugated for the first person in present simple), and the object of the sentence, which is an adverbial phrase "todos los días" (every day).

Based on this example, you can see that building a sentence is rather straightforward. There aren't any complex rules that you need to follow in order to make sense of your ideas. As long as the verb is conjugated properly based on the tense you intend to use, you will be in good shape, moving forward. This is one important point to master.

Now, let us discuss one of the main differences between English and Spanish sentence formation.

Sentences Without Subject

Earlier, we talked about how it is possible to omit the subject of a sentence. In fact, it is quite common to do this, so long as it is clear about who or what you are referring to. If you omit the subject, but it is unclear who the person you are referring, then you might cause confusion in your interlocutor.

Consider this example:

- Trabajo en una oficina. (I work in an office).

The conjugation for "trabajo" makes it clear that you are referring to yourself. In this case, there is no question about who you are talking about. Hence, you can easily omit the subject because your interlocutor will be clear as to who you are referring to.

Please consider this example.

- Trabajo en una oficina. Mi hermano trabaja en un hospital. Mi mejor amiga trabaja desde casa. Es un buen trabajo. (I work in an office. My brother works in a hospital. My best friend works from home. It is a good job.)

This example makes reference to three people. While this is not the issue, the actual issue lies in the "es un buen trabajo" part of the paragraph. What job are you talking about? Whose job are you referring to?

If you base your assumptions on logic, you could infer that the job you are referring to is the last one mentioned; that is, your best friend's. However, if you are actually referring to your own job or that of your brother's, then you will quickly confuse your interlocutor.

Here is a clearer version:

- Trabajo en una oficina. Mi hermano trabaja en un hospital. Mi mejor amiga trabaja desde casa. Mi trabajo es bueno. (I work in an office. My brother works in a hospital. My best friend works from home. My job is good.)

As you can see, it is perfectly fine to refer to an earlier point in the paragraph. As long as you make this clear, you should have no worries about con fusing your interlocutor. Nevertheless, be on the lookout in case the folks with whom you speak commit this error. While they may do it involuntarily, it may confuse you.

In that case, you can just seek clarification by using questions such as:

- ¿Cuál trabajo? (Which job?)
- ¿Tu trabajo o el de tu hermano?) (Your job or your brother's?)
- ¿El trabajo de quién? (Whose job?)

There is no need to feel embarrassed when asking for clarification. Spanish culture does not frown upon asking questions. In fact, asking for clarification can be used to show genuine interest in the conversation. So, don't be afraid to ask for more information if you are not clear on something being said.

Another important aspect of sentence formation is negatives.

Negative Sentences

Earlier, we mentioned the use of "no" in order to build negatives. This is the case, as Spanish does not use any special auxiliaries to build negative sentences. In fact, you can simply use "no" in a regular, affirmative statement, and you should be good to go. But, there is one catch: the use of "no" needs to be in the right spot.

Let us illustrate with a couple of sentences:

- Yo no trabajo en una oficina. (I don't work in an office.)
- Yo no estoy trabajando ahora. (I am not working now.)

In both of these examples, you can see that we are using "no," following the subject and preceding the verb. This is the correct placement of "no." If you happen to place it anywhere else, then it might lead to potential confusion.

In addition, you can omit the subject of the sentence. That would look something like this:

- No trabajo en una oficina. (I don't work in an office.)

- No estoy trabajando ahora. (I am not working now.)

In this case, "no" becomes the first word of the sentence as it is indicating the negation straight away. So, as long as you place "no" before the verb, you will be making a meaningful sentence.

When responding to questions, it is optional to use "no" at the beginning of your reply, or just jump right into the reply itself. Consider this question:

- ¿Quieres un café? (Do you want a coffee?)
    - No, gracias. (No, thank you).
    - No me gusta el café, gracias. (I don't like coffee, thank you.)
    - No tomo café, gracias. (I don't drink coffee, thank you.)

In these examples, you can simply reply using "no." This makes for a much simpler way of replying in the negative form.

One other important aspect of sentence formation in Spanish is the use of time expressions.

Time Expressions

You will find that Spanish speakers use time expressions, either at the beginning or the end of a sentence. This can be somewhat confusing, given the fact that English assigns a specific placement for time expressions. In essence, the placement of time expressions in Spanish depends on what the speaker is trying to get across. For example, the speaker might be more concerned about emphasizing the time expression itself. As such, that would warrant the speaker to place it at the beginning of the sentence. In other cases, the time expression itself might not be as important. So, that might motivate the speaker to place it at the end of the sentence.

Let's have a look at some examples.

- Hoy es mi cumpleaños. (Today is my birthday.)
- Mi cumpleaños es hoy. (My birthda is today.)
- Mañana trabajamos desde casa. (Tomorrow, we work from home.)
- Trabajamos desde casa mañana. (We work from home tomorrow.)
- Ella viaja la próxima semana. (She travels next week.)
- La próxima semana ella viaja. (Next week, she travels.)

In the above examples, you can see how the placement of the time expression can come at either the beginning or the end of the sentence. This illustrates how Spanish syntax is rather flexible. While there is a proper word order that needs to be followed, the main takeaway from this point is that even if you get the word order wrong, you should still be able to get meaning across.

So, don't worry too much about getting the exact word order right since Spanish gives you the opportunity to play around with the placement of words and adverbial phrases.

However, there is one caveat. When you use the subject and verb in a sentence, make sure you don't place them at different points. Consider this example:

- Nosotros mañana viajamos. (We tomorrow travel)

In this example, the time expression "mañana" was inserted in between the verb and the subject. This placement is incorrect. While the insertion of "no," as in, "nosotros no viajamos" makes sense, the use of the time expression would be incorrect. While it is still possible that your interlocutor will get the message, it would simply sound strange and out of place. So, do take care to ensure that you don't insert time expressions in this location.

Overall, making sentences in Spanish is rather straightforward. The most complex part about it is getting the right verb conjugation. But with the guidelines we have presented in this book, you are well on your way go getting the right conjugations. As you gain more practice and experience, you will also be able to make the most of your language skills. As such, you will be able to construct solid sentences in no time.

Chapter 17: The Imperative and Subjunctive Moods

Indicative Mood

In general, Spanish speakers use the indicative mood when engaging in regular conversation. An indicative mood is a form used to provide information, state facts, and even express opinions in the past, present, future, and conditionals.

As such, the use of the indicative mood is the most commonly used form to express meaning. Thus far, we have focused on the indicative mood. The tenses that we have discussed are all centered on this mood.

Consider this example:

- Estoy viendo la televisión. (I am watching television.)

This example illustrates how you can express a fact. The fact in this example is that you are watching television.

This seems pretty straightforward, right?

Indeed, the indicative mood is the most commonly used mood in regular conversation. However, things change somewhat when you move away from the indicative mood and enter the subjunctive.

Subjunctive Mood

You probably have not heard of the subjunctive mood, as it is not a common topic in English classes. However, it is widely used in Spanish. In fact, the subjunctive is used about as much as the indicative mood. It is one of the nuances that native Spanish speakers develop more out of custom and habit than out of sheer linguistic proficiency.

You are probably wondering what the subjunctive mood is and how its use translates to the English language.

The subjunctive mood is essentially used to express wishes, obligation, necessity, desires, and doubt. Consequently, we are moving away from expressing facts and opinions to a bit of a gray area in which we are not necessarily talking about things that are clear-cut.

As such, the subjunctive is used any time you move away from "real" situations and into situations that reflect conditions, which are not always true at the moment. Hence, desires, wishes, and doubt fall perfectly into this category.

So, let us delve more into the expression of wishes and desires. In this case, you are referring to situations where you would like something to happen but may not necessarily have the ability to make it happen at the time of speaking or may seem unlikely at some point. You can even express situations that are completely unreal.

For instance, you might be thinking about situations where you wish you had millions of dollars or that you could change something that is impossible to change. These circumstances, given the fact that you are not talking about a fact, would fall into the realm of the subjunctive.

Here are some expressions that generally accompany the subjunctive:

- Desear que (to wish that)
- Esperar que (to hope that)
- Exigir que (to demand that)
- Mandar que (to order that)
- Ordenar que (to order that)
- Pedir que (to ask that)
- Preferir que (to prefer that)
- Querer que (to want that)

Notice that we are talking about expressions that refer to things that you wish, hope, and prefer to happen. Also, you can see how there are actions that you can order or demand to be done. Now, it should be noted that these are not direct orders or requests. When you make a request using the subjunctive form, you are either requesting that something be done as a result of a condition being met, or you are simply trying to be much more polite about it.

The subjunctive can also be used to talk about emotions or reactions to certain situations. The underlying reason for the use of the subjunctive when expressing reactions and emotions is the use of the expression "es + adjective + que." This expression, when used to express emotions or reactions, is a signal that you are using the subjunctive form.

Here are some examples of this construction:

- Es absurdo que (it is absurd that)
- Es bonito que (it is nice that)
- Es Bueno que (it is good that)
- Es fundamental que (it is essential that)
- Es importante que (it is important that)
- Es inútil que (it is useless that)
- Es justo que (it is fair that)
- Es triste que (it is sad that)
- Es urgente que (it is urgent that)
- Me encanta que (I love that)
- Me gusta que (I like that)
- Me molesta que (it bothers me that)
- Me sorprende que (it surprises me that)

Notice how these constructions all represent ideas and feelings, which may not necessarily be true at the time of speaking. While you might be talking about something that is very much present at the time of speaking, you might also be talking about something that hasn't even happened yet.

Consider this example:

- Es importante llegar a tiempo. (It is important to get there on time.)

In this example, the subjunctive form in Spanish matches up quite well with the subjunctive form in English. While the use of the subjunctive in English isn't nearly as prevalent as it is in Spanish, the previous example makes a great case forusing this form in both languages.

One other case in which the subjunctive is used is when the speaker is expressing doubt or disbelief. The following expressions are characteristic of this case.

- No creer que (not to believe that)
- Dudar que (doubt that)
- No opinar que (not to think that)
- No pensar que (not to thinkthat)

You can also use the following conjunctions with the subjunctive mood.

- A fin de que (in order to)
- A menos que (unless)
- Antes de que (before that)
- Sin que (without)
- Con tal de que (provided that)
- Ojalá (hopefully)
- Quizá (maybe)
- Para que (so that)
- Tal vez (perhaps)

Below are words pertaining to time that can also be used:

- Cuando (when)
- En cuanto (as soon as)
- Hasta que (until)
- Después de que (after)
- Tan pronto como (as soon as)

As you can see, there is a good deal of expressions that signal the use of the subjunctive. As you gain more experience with the subjunctive, you will automatically begin to recognize what expression or part of speech prompts the subjunctive form usage. So, it certainly pays to do your homework.

Imperative Mood

The other mood used in Spanish is the imperative mood. In short, the imperative is used to give direct orders and commands. In English, the imperative allows the speaker to omit the use of the subject as it is implied that the subject of a command is "you." The same rule applies in Spanish.

Now, you might be wondering what differences there would be between the use of the imperative mood and commands given in the subjunctive. First of all, orders and requests given in the subjunctive can be directed at anyone. In the case of the imperative, the orders and commands given are directed specifically to "you."

As with the subjunctive, verb conjugation changes to reflect the difference in mood. Here is a general overview of such changes in conjugation.

With regular AR verbs, you can use the following rule of thumb.

- Verb: hablar (to speak)
    - (tú) habla – no hables (negative form)
    - (usted) hable
    - (nosotros) hablemos
    - (ustedes) hablen

Notice how the verb conjugation changes in the endings given to the verb. Also, the subject is placed in parentheses as it is not used when actually saying such phrases, but we have included them to illustrate the subject we are referring to.

The conjugation of the regular IR verbs, as well as ER verbs, can be viewed as follows:

- Verb: comer (to eat)
    - (tú) come / no comas (negative form)
    - (usted) coma
    - (nosotros) comamos
    - (ustedes) coman

Once again, you can see how the verb endings reflect a variation in the regular conjugation. As you become familiar with this form, you will notice how straightforward it actually is. The challenge, of course, is to recall the proper endings in this mood.

There are also irregular verbs that can be used in the imperative mood. So, here are the most common commands used:

- Di (say)
- Haz (do)
- Pon (put)
- Sal (come out)
- Sé (be)
- Ten (have)
- Ve (go)
- Ven (come here)

Consider these examples:

- Di algo (say something)
- Haz un esfuerzo (make an effort)
- Pon tu nombre (put your name)
- Sal a jugar (come out to play)
- Sé honesto (be honest)

- Ten paciencia (have patience)
- Ve a dormir (go to sleept)
- Ven conmigo (come here with me)

These examples all illustrate commands that you can express using the imperative mood. Also, they use the (tú) form. So, you can easily use them whenever you are asking your interlocutor to carry out an action at any given point.

Ultimately, the use of the indicative, subjunctive, and imperative all boils down to the situation where you find yourself communicating. Consequently, you can use any of these moods to get your message across effectively. So, do take the time to go over the various moods so that you can recognize them.

Chapter 18: Making Comparisons

The basic structure for the comparative form in Spanish is rather straightforward. As such, you can quickly begin to put it into practice in order to express your ideas.

In essence, comparisons boil down to the use of adjectives to compare two or more objects or people. This structure is evidenced by the "más + adjective + que" expression. This expression takes the adjective, which is the focal point of the comparison.

Comparative Form

It is important to keep in mind that this comparison is about two items. The adjective in question is meant to compare the two items that are contrasted. Virtually any adjective can be used in this case. So, let's consider some examples of this structure:

- Roberto es más alto que Diego. (Roberto is taller than Diego.)

In this example, we are using the verb "ser" since we are discussing permanent conditions. After all, height is a rather permanent condition that cannot be altered. Therefore, we generally use the verb "ser" to compare and contrast the characteristics of individual items. Next, we have "más" (more) and the adjective in question. "Alto" (tall) agrees in both gender and number. That means if the items in question are in singular form or plural, the adjective must reflect this difference. This is also the case if the items are feminine or masculine. Then, "que" introduces the second item in question.

Let's consider the following example to illustrate agreement in terms of both number and gender.

- Las niñas son más rápidas que los niños. (Girls are faster than boys.)

In this example, we are comparing two groups, that is, girls and boys. As such, "niñas" (girls) is plural. This means that the adjective "rápidas" (fast) must agree both in terms of number and gender. This is a key point to keep in mind as this is applicable to all cases. Nevertheless, we are still comparing two items, even if they are actually a number of items grouped into a single one.

Similarity

If you would like to indicate that two items are the same or not, you can use this expression: "igual que" (same as).

With this expression, you are indicating that two items are the same. For instance: "un libro digital es igual que un libro físico" (a digital book is the same as a physical book.) In this example, you are making clear that both items are the same; that is, there is no difference between them.

Now, consider this situation:

- "Un libro digital no es igual que un libro físico" (A digital book is not the same as a physical book.)

In this example, you are simply saying that both items are different. While you are not specifying where the difference lies, you are stating that the items in question do not have the same characteristics.

So, you can use this structure to simply make a point that two items or groups of items are the same or different. Ultimately, your use of this structure is intended to mark the difference or similarity between the items in question.

Superlative Form

When you are comparing more than two items, you can use the superlative form. This form indicates that there is one item that is "more" or "less" than the rest. This form can be used anytime you are comparing any number of items in excess of two.

Consider the following example:

- Alejandra es la mejor estudiante de quinto grado. (Alejandra is the best student of the 5th graders.)

In this example, you are saying that "Alejandra" is the best student out of all the students in Grade 5. While the number of students isn't known (at least from simply reading the statement), it is clear that "Alejandra" is the best one of all. This implies that there are at least three students in the class.

You can even use this form to refer to an immense number of objects. For instance:

- Los agujeros negros son los objetos más grandes del universo. (Black holes are the largest objects in the universe).

In this case, we are comparing the vast number of objects in the universe. So, given the fact that there is an unfathomable number of objects out there, it is a good idea to use the superlative form to make such a generalization.

Consequently, you can see that the main difference lies in the use of "el/la" or "los/las." This is what underscores the use of the superlative form. Consider this other example:

- El Ferrari es el auto más costoso. (The Ferrari is the most expensive)

In this example, you are making it clear that it is "the most expensive," thereby making proper use of the superlative form. However, keep in mind that this form needs to agree in both number and gender. So, "los agujeros negros" is masculine plural. By the same token, "el Ferrari" is masculine singular.

Of course, you could also make other types of generalizations that are intended to reflect an opinion. The example, "Laura es la chica más bella del mundo" (Laura is the most beautiful girl in the world) is intended to reflect a personal opinion more than anything else. As such, you can use this form to reflect your personal opinions and beliefs about a person or object.

In this case, we are making an agreement with a singular feminine noun, that is, "Laura." As you gain more practice with this form, you will be able to recognize quickly the difference that lies among the various nouns and their corresponding agreements.

Comparison of Verbs

One other use of the comparative and superlative forms lies in the comparison of verbs. Technically speaking, this comparison requires the use of adverbs since you would be describing an action. Nevertheless, the structure and use of adjectives remain the same.

Consider the following examples:

- Fernando juega fútbol mejor que Pablo. (Fernando plays soccer better than Pablo)
- Nancy habla más despacio que Patricia. (Nancy speaks slower than Patricia)
- Los niños comen menos que los adultos. (Kids eat less than adults)
- Los dólares valen más que los pesos. (Dollars are worth more than pesos)
- Las computadoras trabajan más eficientemente que las máquinas de escribir. (Computers work more efficiently than typewriters)

In these examples, we can see how the comparison among objects is focused on the way certain actions are done, as opposed to the characteristics of these items themselves. Consequently, you can use the same form, though instead of using the verb "ser," you can virtually useany verb that you wish to take into account.

Notice in the sentence, "Las computadoras trabajan más eficientemente que las máquinas de escribir," where we are using the adverb "eficientemente" (efficiently) to highlight the difference between the two items. Thus, you can virtually use any adjective or adverb to state your comparisons.

Also, keep in mind that all adjectives and adverbs are preceded by "más" (more) or "menos" (less). Hence, there is no need for transformations, such as "nice" into "nicer." This makes expressing comparisons much more straightforward as compared to English.

Chapter 19: Short Stories

In this chapter, we are presenting five short stories that you can read to practice the language which we have discussed throughout this book. Each story has its own topic, where important vocabulary is presented before the story. Then, you have the story, which you can read at your own leisure.

Once you have gotten through the story, you will find some questions about it. Each of the questions is intended to help you practice both reading comprehension and grammar skills. The responses to these questions are based on the text itself. Also, we have included suggested answers in order to provide you with some guidance.

So, do take the time to go over these questions; they will help you get the most out of the various topics, which we have covered in this volume. Furthermore, you can see the language in a real-life context. Indeed, this is a great combination.

Most importantly, you can begin to practice the language that we have discussed throughout this book in an engaging manner. As such, here is a suggested methodology that you can apply to the study of these short stories.

1. First, please review the vocabulary presented at the beginning of the story. The words in that vocabulary have been selected in order to help you warm up for the content in the story. You will find both the Spanish and English words in the list. That way, you won't have to guess their meaning. You can read through the list, and make a note of the words that you find new or challenging.
2. Next, read through the story, paragraph by paragraph. Since you will find the Spanish and English version, you will be able to visualize the structures and conjugations that we have studied throughout this volume. That way, you will be able to make a mental note of the way each structure is presented in real-life. This makes learning grammar and sentence structure a lot more digestible.
3. Then, go through every one of the paragraphs. When you reach the end of the story, go back to any parts that you feel weren't clear or perhaps you have questions about. You can focus on these parts so that you can get the extra practice that you need. Once you feel comfortable with the entire story, you can then move on to the questions.
4. The questions following the story are both meant to test your reading comprehension and give you an opportunity to practice your writing skills. This exercise will provide you with the chance to use your imagination as it pertains to writing skills.
5. Finally, the suggested responses at the end of the story are meant to serve as a guide. So, you can compare your own answers to the suggested ones. Of course, these are only suggested answers. That means you can very well come up with your own answers according to the passage that you have read.

We have some tips that will help you get the most out of these stories based on the methodology suggested:

- Don't feel that you need to get through the entire story in one session. In fact, each story has been designed so that you can take one paragraph at a time. Also, you can begin with the vocabulary and then take each paragraph as time allows you. That way, you won't feel like you have been interrupted. If anything, you will be able to pick up with where you left off.
- Take your time. There is no need to rush through the stories or any part of this book. This volume can very well serve you as a reference guide. That way, you can always go back to it whenever you have the need to doso.
- Try your best to set aside a specific amount of time each day for study with this book. Even 10 or 15 minutes a day is enough to get you into the habit of daily practice. Since practice is the best way in which you can improve your skills, you will soon find that getting into a groove is not nearly as hard as you thought it would be. So, do try to make some time during a break at work, your daily commute, or even before bedtime to go through parts of each story or any other part of this book. We are sure that you will not only find it enjoyable but also productive.

We hope you enjoy every one of these stories. They have been carefully crafted to provide you with practice and meaningful experience.

Story #1: Un nuevo empleo / A New Job

Vocabulario Importante	Important Vocabulary
contador	accountant
departamento	apartment
películas de acción	action movies
experiencia	experience
universidad	university
además	in addition
viajar	travel
sueño	dream
disciplina	discipline
comprar	buy
empleo	job
optimista	optimistic

Francisco es el nuevo **contador** de la empresa "La Mejor." Él es un chico joven. Tiene veintisiete años. Es de Nueva York y vive en un **departamento** con su perro Bruno. Francisco le gusta jugar fútbol y ver **películas de acción** en los fines de semana.

Francisco is the new **accountant** at the company "La Mejor." He is a young guy. He is twenty-seven years old. He is from New York and lives in an **apartment** with his dog, Bruno. Francisco likes to play soccer and watch **action movies** on the weekends.

Francisco tiene cinco años de **experiencia**. Actualmente, está estudiando en la **universidad**. Está en el último año de su carrera. Francisco espera graduarse el próximo año. **Además**, tiene muchos planes para el futuro.

Francisco has five years of **experience**. Currently, he is studying at the **university**. He is in the last year of his course of study. Francisco hopes to graduate next year. **In addition**, he has many plans for the future.

Primero, Francisco desea **viajar** por Europa. Este es un **sueño** para él. Francisco desea conocer París, Londres y Madrid. El segundo plan que tiene es comprar un coche nuevo. Él sabe que con su trabajo y un poco de **disciplina**, él puede comprar el coche que quiere. El tercer plan que tiene es **comprar** su propio departamento. Para esto, él necesita mucho dinero, pero está dedicado a lograrlo.

First, Francisco wants to **travel** to Europe. This is a **dream** for him. Francisco wants to know Paris, London, and Madrid. The second plan he has is to buy a new car. He knows that with his work and a little **discipline**, he can buy the car he wants. The third plan that he has is to **buy** his own apartment. To do this, he needs a lot of money, but he is dedicated to achieving it.

Hoy es el primer día de su nuevo **empleo**. Él está seguro de que es un buen trabajador y que sus resultados son buenos. Francisco está muy **optimista** del futuro que tiene en su nuevo puesto de trabajo. Le deseamos todo lo mejor a Francisco con sus planes.

Today is the first day of his new **job**. He is sure that he is a good worker and that his results are good. Francisco is very **optimistic** about the future that he has in his new job. We wish Francisco all the best with his plans.

Preguntas sobre la historia	**Questions about the story**
¿Quién es Francisco?	Who is Francisco?
¿En qué empresa trabaja?	In what company does he work?
¿Con quién vive Francisco?	Who does Francisco live with?
¿Qué desea Francisco?	What does Francisco want?
¿Qué quiere Francisco comprar?	What does Francisco want to buy?

Respuestas sugeridas	**Suggested responses**
¿Quién es Francisco?	Who is Francisco?
Es un chico joven de veintiocho años. Es contador en una empresa.	He is a young guy. He is twenty-eight years old. He works in a company.
¿En qué empresa trabaja?	In what company does he work?
Él trabaja en la empresa "La Mejor."	He works at the company "La Mejor."
¿Con quién vive Francisco?	Who does Francisco live with?
Francisco vive con su perro Bruno.	Francisco lives with his dog, Bruno.
¿Qué desea Francisco?	What does Francisco want?
Él desea viajar a Europa.	He wants to travel to Europe.
¿Qué quiere Francisco comprar?	What does Francisco want to buy?
Él quiere comprar un coche y un departamento nuevo.	He wants to buy a car and a new apartment.

Story #2: Como hacer nuevos amigos / How to Make New Friends

Vocabulario Importante	Important Vocabulary
oportunidad	opportunity
algunas	some
presentarte	introduce yourself
útiles	useful
también	also
conversación	conversation
consiste	involves
apropiadamente	appropriately
preguntas	questions
amable	kind
tímidas	shy
consejos	tips

Cuando conoces a una persona nueva, tienes una **oportunidad** de hacer un nuevo amigo. Por eso es que debes conocer **algunas** frases importantes que puedes utilizar para **presentarte** y conocer mejor a tu nuevo amigo.

Frases como, "¿cuál es tu nombre?" y "¿de dónde eres?" son muy **útiles** para conocer mejor a tus nuevos amigos. **También** puedes usar frases como, "mi nombre es _____" y "soy de ___." Con estas frases, puedes iniciar una buena **conversación**.

Una buena conversación **consiste** en hacer **preguntas** interesantes y responder **apropiadamente**. Si haces buenas preguntas y escuchas a tu nuevo amigo, es seguro que la conversación es positiva. De lo contrario, puede parecer aburrido. Por eso es muy importante ser amigable, atento y **amable**.

Las personas **tímidas** tienen problemas para hacer amigos algunas veces. Cuando te sientes nervioso al conocer a una persona nueva, simplemente debes

When you meet a new person, you have an **opportunity** to make a new friend. That's why you should know **some** important phrases that you can use to **introduce yourself** and get to know your new friend better.

Phrases like, "what's your name?" and "where are you from?" are very **useful** for getting to know your new friends better. You can **also** use phrases such as, "My name is ____" and "I am from _____." With these phrases, you can start a good **conversation**.

A good conversation **involves** asking interesting **questions** and answering them **appropriately**. If you ask good questions and listen to your new friend, it is certain that the conversation is positive. Otherwise, you may seem bored. That is why it is very important to be friendly, attentive, and kind.

Shy people have trouble making friends sometimes. When you feel nervous when meeting a new person, you should simply take a deep breath and greet the person

respirar profundo y saludar a la persona cordialmente. Una sonrisa también es una buena manera de iniciar una conversación. También es buena idea aprender el nombre de tu nuevo amigo. Siempre es buena idea llamar a las personas por su nombre. Así, les puedes mostrar que pones atención y estás interesado en conocerlos bien.

cordially. A smile is also a good way to start a conversation. It is also a good idea to learn the name of your new friend. It is always a good idea to call people by their name. Thus, you can show them that you pay attention and are interested in knowing them well.

Con estos **consejos**, puedes hacer amigos rápidamente. No necesitas habilidades especiales. Solo necesitas ser una persona auténtica. De esa manera, siempre tienes una buena oportunidad para conocer nuevas personas y hacer amigos interesantes.

With these **tips**, you can make friends quickly. You do not need special skills. You just need to be an authentic person. That way, you always have a good opportunity to meet new people and make interesting friends.

Preguntas sobre la historia	**Questions about the story**
¿Qué debes hacer cuando conoces a una persona nueva? ____________________ ____________________	What should you do when you meet a new person? ____________________ ____________________
¿Cuáles frases puedes utilizar? ____________________ ____________________	What phrases can you use? ____________________ ____________________
¿En qué consiste una buena conversación? ____________________ ____________________	What does a good conversation involve? ____________________ ____________________
¿Qué es una buena idea cuando conoces a una persona nueva? ____________________ ____________________	What is a good idea when you meet a new person? ____________________ ____________________
¿Qué necesitas para hacer amigos??	What do you need to make new friends?

Respuestas sugeridas	Suggested responses
¿Qué debes hacer cuando conoces a una persona nueva?	What should you do when you meet a new person?
Debe hacer preguntas interesantes sobre una persona nueva.	You should ask interesting questions about a new person.
¿Cuáles frases puedes utilizar?	What phrases can you use?
Puedes usar frases como "¿cuál es tu nombre?" y "¿de dónde eres?"	You can use phrases such as, "what's your name?" and "where are you from?"
¿En qué consiste una buena conversación?	What does a good conversation involve?
Una buena conversación consiste en poner atención a tu nuevo amigo.	A good conversation involves paying attention to your new friend.
¿Qué es una buena idea cuando conoces a una persona nueva?	What is a good idea when you meet a new person?
Es una buena idea recordar el nombre de tu nuevo amigo.	It is a good idea to remember your new friends' name.
¿Qué necesitas para hacer amigos?	What do you need to make new friends?
No necesitas nada especial, solo ser una persona auténtica.	You don't need anything special; just being an authentic person.

Story #3: Mi deporte favorito / My Favorite Sport

Vocabulario Importante	Important Vocabulary
activa	active
no puedo	can't
natación	swimming
especialmente	especially
usualmente	usually
después	after
gimnasio	gym
algunas veces	sometimes
tan bonito	such a nice
saludablemente	healthy
próximo	next
difícil	difficult

Soy una persona **activa**. Me gusta el ejercicio y los deportes. **No puedo** vivir sin hacer ejercicio y practicar deportes. Esto me hace sentir bien. Me siento motivada para trabajar y estudiar.

I'm an **active** person. I like exercising and sports. I **can't** live without exercising and playing sports. This makes me feel good. I feel motivated to work and study.

Mi deporte favorito es la **natación**. También me gusta correr y jugar tenis, pero la natación es mi deporte favorito. Disfruto mucho estar en el agua. El agua se siente excelente **especialmente** cuando hace mucho calor.

My favorite sport is **swimming**. I also like to run and play tennis, but swimming is my favorite sport. I really enjoy being in the water. The water feels excellent, **especially** when it is very hot.

Voy a nadar tres veces por semana. **Usualmente** voy martes, jueves y sábado. Los demás días, voy al gimnasio **después** de mi trabajo. Tengo tiempo para ir una o dos horas al **gimnasio** los lunes y miércoles.

I go swimming three times a week. I **usually** go on Tuesday, Thursday, and Saturday. On the other days of the week, I go to the gym **after** work. I have time to go, for an hour or two, to the **gym** on Mondays and Wednesdays.

Algunas veces, tengo oportunidad de jugar tenis con mis amigos. Podemos jugar tenis los días domingo. El tenis es un deporte **tan bonito**. El tenis es más bonito que el fútbol. Es un gran ejercicio.

Sometimes, I have the opportunity to play tennis with my friends. We can play tennis on Sunday. Tennis is **such a beautiful** sport. Tennis is more beautiful than football. It is a great exercise.

También me gusta comer **saludablemente**. Siempre hay verduras y frutas en mis comidas. También agrego

I also like to eat **healthy**. There are always veggies and fruits in my meals. I also add chicken and fish in any meal that I eat. I

pollo y pescado cuando cocino las comidas. Me importa mucho estar en forma y saludable. Una vida saludable es esencial para vivir felizmente.

care a lot about being fit and healthy. A healthy life is essential to living happily.

El **próximo** mes espero viajar a los Estados Unidos. Hay muchas montañas para escalar. Este es un deporte que quiero intentar. Sé que es **difícil**, pero es un reto que deseo superar. Yo sé que con esfuerzo puedo hacer cualquier cosa.

Next month, I hope to travel to the United States. There are many mountains to climb. This is a sport that I want to try. I know it's **difficult**, but it's a challenge that I want to overcome. I know that with effort, I can do anything.

Y tú, ¿cuál es tu deporte favorito?

And you, what is your favorite sport?

Preguntas sobre la historia

Questions about the story

¿Cuál es mi deporte favorito?	What is my favorite sport?
¿Cuándo es el mejor momento para hacer mi deporte favorito?	When is the best time to do my favorite sport?
¿Qué alimentos me gusta comer?	What foods do I like eating?
¿En qué consiste mi dieta?	What does my diet involve?
¿Cuándo visito los Estados Unidos?	When do I visit the United States?

Respuestas sugeridas	**Suggested responses**
¿Cuál es mi deporte favorito?	What is my favorite sport?
Mi deporte favorito es la natación.	My favorite sport is swimming.
¿Cuándo es el mejor momento para hacer mi deporte favorito?	When is the best time to do your favorite sport?
Disfruto nadar cuando hace mucho calor.	I enjoy swimming when it is very hot.
¿Qué alimentos me gusta comer?	What foods do I like eating?
Me gusta comer comidas saludables.	I like eating healthy meals.
¿En qué consiste mi dieta?	What does my diet involve?
Mi dieta consiste en comida saludable como frutas y vegetales.	My diet involves healthy food, like fruits and vegetables.
¿Cuándo visito los Estados Unidos?	When do I visit the United States?
Viajaré a los Estados Unidos el próximo mes.	I will travel next month to the United States.

Story #4: Comer en un restaurante / Eating in a Restaurant

Vocabulario Importante	**Important Vocabulary**
sirven	serve
prácticos	practical
dinero	money
comida rápida	fast food
de hecho	in fact
todos los días	every day
ingredientes	ingredients
ensaladas	salads
grasa	fat
alta calidad	high quality
ambiente	atmosphere
comida casera	homemade food

Los restaurantes **sirven** todo tipo de comidas. Algunos restaurantes sirven comida rápida como pizza, hamburguesas, y tacos. Estos restaurantes están por todas partes. Son **prácticos** y no tienes que gastar mucho **dinero** para comer bastantes.

Restaurants **serve** all kinds of meals. Some restaurants serve fast food, such as pizza, hamburgers, and tacos. These restaurants are everywhere. They are **practical**, and you don't have to spend a lot of **money** to eat a lot.

Pero, la **comida rápida** no siempre es saludable. **De hecho**, la comida rápida puede ser muy mala para la salud. Por eso debes cuidar de no comer mucha comida rápida. Lo mejor es no comer este tipo de comida **todos los días**.

But **fast food** is not always healthy. **In fact**, fast food can be very bad for your health. That is why you should take care not to eat too much fast food. It is best not to eat this type of food **every day**.

Otro tipo de restaurantes sirven comida más saludable. Estos restaurantes preparan la comida con **ingredientes** frescos y ofrecen menús para personas que quieren perder peso. Puedes comer **ensaladas**, frutas y comida preparada sin **grasa**. Esta es comida nutritiva pero deliciosa.

Other restaurants serve healthier food. These restaurants prepare food with fresh **ingredients** and offer menus for people who want to lose weight. You can eat **salads**, fruits, and food prepared without fat. This is nutritious but delicious food.

Luego, existen restaurantes que sirven comida de **alta calidad**. Pero, estos restaurantes también son caros. Los precios son elevados y el **ambiente** es

Then, there are restaurants that serve **high quality** food. But, these restaurants are also expensive. The prices are high, and the **atmosphere** is very good. In

muy bueno. En estosrestaurantes, puedes probar comida de todo diferentes países del mundo.

these restaurants, you can try food from the different countries of the world.

Finalmente, existen restaurantes que sirven **comida casera**. Este tipo de comida es similar a la comida preparada en casa. Usualmente, es comida local, pero es muy buena. Este tipo de restaurantes son los favoritos de los turistas. No te puedes perder un restaurante de comida casera en tu próximo viaje.

Finally, there are restaurants that serve homemade food. This type of food is similar to food prepared at home. It is usually local food, but it is very good. These types of restaurants are the favorites of tourists. You cannot miss a restaurant that serves homemade food on your next trip.

Preguntas sobre la historia

¿Qué tipo de comida sirven los restaurantes de comida rápida?

____

____

¿Cómo es la comida rápida?

____

____

¿Qué ingredientes se usan en la comida saludable?

____

____

¿Cómo son los restaurantes de alta calidad?

____

____

¿Cómo es la comida casera?

____

____

Questions about the story

What type of food do fast food restaurants serve?

____

____

What is fast food like?

____

____

What ingredients are used in healthy food?

____

____

____

What are high-quality restaurants like?

____

____

What is homemade food like?

____

____

Respuesta sugeridas	Suggested responses
¿Qué tipo de comida sirven los restaurantes de comida rápida?	What type of food do fast food restaurants serve?
Los restaurantes de comida rápida sirven pizza, hamburguesas y tacos.	Fast food restaurants serve pizza, hamburgers, and tacos.
¿Cómo es la comida rápida?	What is fast food like?
La comida rápida es práctica, pero es mala para la salud.	Fast food is practical, but it is bad for your health.
¿Qué ingredientes se usan en la comida saludable?	What ingredients are used in healthy food?
La comida saludable usa ingredientes frescos.	Healthy food uses fresh ingredients.
¿Cómo son los restaurantes de alta calidad?	What are high quality restaurants like?
Los restaurantes de alta calidad son caros y el ambiente es muy bueno.	High quality restaurants are expensive, and the atmosphere is really good.
¿Cómo es la comida casera?	What is homemade food like?
La comida casera es como la comida preparada en casa.	Homemade food is like food prepared at home.

Story #5: De compras en el centro comercial / Shopping at the Mall

Vocabulario Importante	**Important Vocabulary**
edificio	building
tiendas	shops
entre otros	among others
encontrar	find
compras	shopping
estacionamiento	parking lot
vehículos	vehicles
clientes	customers
relacionadas	related
por ejemplo	for example
niños	children
seguramente	surely

Un centro comercial es un **edificio** en donde existen **tiendas** y restaurantes. Las tiendas son negocios donde hay productos que puedes comprar. Estos productos son ropa, zapatos, electrónicos, muebles, libros, **entre otros**.

A shopping mall is a **building** where there are shops and restaurants. Stores are businesses where there are products you can buy. These products are clothes, shoes, electronics, furniture, and books, among others.

Además, puedes **encontrar** restaurantes en un centro comercial. Estos restaurantes pueden ser de comida rápida, o de otro tipo de comida. Muchas personas van de **compras** y luego pasan a un restaurante a comer algo.

In addition, you can **find** restaurants in a mall. These restaurants can be fast food or other kinds of food. Many people go **shopping** and then go to a restaurant to eat something.

En un centro comercial, encuentras un **estacionamiento.** El estacionamiento es el lugar donde los **clientes** del centro comercial dejan sus **vehículos** mientras hacen compras o visitan un restaurante. Existen lugares marcados para cada coche. Normalmente, debes pagar una cantidad de dinero por el uso deestacionamiento.

In a mall, you can find a parking lot. The **parking lot** is the place where mall **customers** leave their **vehicles** while shopping or visiting a restaurant. There are marked places for each car. Normally, you must pay an amount of money for the use of the parking.

Los días en donde más personas visitan los centros comerciales son sábado y domingo. Estos dos días son el fin de semana. Por lo regular, los fines de semana son para actividades que no están

The days where more people visit the malls are on Saturday and Sunday. These two days are the weekend. Usually, weekends are for activities that are not work-**related**. **For example**, they are used to

relacionadas con el trabajo. **Por ejemplo**, se usan para pasar tiempo en familia. Existen muchas actividades en un centro comercial los fines de semana especialmente para **niños**.

spend time with family. There are many activities in a shopping mall on weekends, especially for children.

Seguramente hay un centro comercial cerca de tu casa o tu trabajo. Puedes ir con tu familiar a disfrutar de un buen momento, comprar artículos a buenos precios, y salir de la rutina, al menos durante el fin de semana.

Surely, there is a mall near your home or your place of work. You can go with your family to have a good time, buy items at good prices, and break your usual routine, at least during the weekend.

Preguntas sobre la historia	**Questions about the story**
¿Qué es un centro comercial? ____________________ ____________________	What is a shopping mall? ____________________ ____________________
¿Qué productos puedes comprar en un centro comercial? ____________________ ____________________	What products can you buy in a shopping mall? ____________________ ____________________
¿Qué es el estacionamiento? ____________________ ____________________	What is the parking lot? ____________________ ____________________
¿Qué días visitan los clientes el centro comercial? ____________________ ____________________	What days do customers visit the shopping mall? ____________________ ____________________
¿Qué puedes hacer en un centro comercial? ____________________ ____________________	What can you do at a shopping mall? ____________________ ____________________

Respuestas sugeridas	**Suggested responses**
¿Qué es un centro comercial?	What is a shopping mall?
Es un edificio con muchas tiendas y restaurantes.	It is a building with many shops and restaurants.
¿Qué productos puedes comprar en un centro comercial?	What products can you buy in a shopping mall?
Puedes comprar ropa, zapatos, electrónicos y libros entre otros.	You can buy clothes, shoes, electronics, and books among other
¿Qué es el estacionamiento?	What is the parking lot?
Es el lugar en donde los clientes estacionan sus vehículos.	It is the place where customers park their vehicles.
¿Qué días visitan los clientes el centro comercial?	What days do customers visit the shopping mall?
Los días que los clientes visitan el centro comercial son los sábado y domingo.	The days that customers visit the shopping mall are Saturday and Sunday.
¿Qué puedes hacer en un centro comercial?	What can you do at a shopping mall?
Puedes hacer las compras o comer en un restaurante.	You can do shopping or eat in a restaurant.

Conclusion

We are at the end of this journey into the world of Spanish. We are certain that you have learned much about the Spanish language, how it works, and how you can use it to your advantage. The most important thing is that you got through the entire book. This means that you are committed to learning Spanish.

Of course, learning a language is not easy. It takes time and dedication. Total mastery of language is a skill that is crafted over years of practice and experience. Nevertheless, we all need to start somewhere. If you never take that first step, you will never be able to attain a level of proficiency with which you are comfortable.

So, we would certainly encourage you to keep reviewing and practicing the content in this book. It has been designed in such a way that each time you go through a section or chapter, you will always find something new to think about. This is the type of exercise that will help you hone your skills and further develop your abilities.

At this point, what is the next step?

First of all, go back and review any parts that you feel were challenging or particularly interesting. By reviewing a part of this book, or even the entire volume itself, you will find that it will help you reinforce your understanding of each topic. This will then allow you to springboard into more advanced topics.

Next, be sure to take as many notes as you need to. Note-taking will help you to fixate language in your mind. In short, writing things down on paper is a great way to force your brain to take permanent note of the language you have learned. What this means is that you are exercising the various skills that are involved in the learning process. Consequently, you will get as much as you can out of this book.

Then, setting up a daily practice schedule will help you to build consistency and momentum in your learning. Often, we don't have much time to spare. Yet, there is always some way where you can spare 10 or 15 minutes a day. This could mean taking some time away from your lunchtime, using your commute, or even taking a few minutes before going to bed. It doesn't matter when you are able to make time. What does matter is that you do it. You will find that as you make more time to study, you will build a habit that will eventually lead you to become consistent in your progress. Before you know it, you will begin to see results.

Also, finding Spanish-speaking friends is a great way to test your new language skills. It is very likely that any Spanish-speaking friends that you might have will be more than willing to help you practice what you have learned in this book. Also, this type of practice and exposure will enable you to play with the language so that you can become comfortable with going off-script. This will allow you to truly begin to communicate through the use of what you have actually learned.

If you are planning on traveling, you will find that the language presented in this book will be invaluable as you navigate your way through the various places and situations that you will encounter. Best of all, you will have the opportunity to put yourself to the test. There is an undeniable feeling of satisfaction that comes when you are able to communicate in a foreign language.

We are confident that you found the content in this book useful in any situation. In fact, don't be surprised if you get caught in learning Spanish. You might even choose to pursue your learning even further.

In that case, do check out the subsequent volumes in this series. You will find that they are intended to help you deepen your knowledge and understanding of the Spanish language in such a way that you will be truly on your way to mastering Spanish communication skills.

So, thank you for taking the time to read this book. There are plenty of options out there which claim to teach you Spanish in a short period of time. Unfortunately, some of those courses under-deliver in terms of value, while others turn out to be a costly experience.

If you have found this book useful and informative, do tell your friends, colleagues, and family members. Perhaps they have been looking for a viable alternative to learn Spanish. In that case, they will hopefully get as much out of this book as you have.

Thank you once again. See you in the next volume.

Spanish Short Stories for Beginners:

21 Entertaining Short Stories to Learn Spanish and Develop Your Vocabulary the Fun Way!

Introduction

Thank you for purchasing, "*Spanish Short Stories for Beginners: 21 Entertaining Short Stories to Learn Spanish and Develop Your Vocabulary the Fun Way!*"

If you are looking for a fun and easy way to develop your Spanish skills, then you have come to the right place. In this volume, you will find the best way to develop your Spanish skills in no time.

Often, it can be complicated for language learners to find the right type of materials with which to learn a new language and practice what they already know. In fact, there is a myriad of materials out there to choose from.

So, the challenge becomes: where to begin.

The truth is that there are many courses and materials out there, claiming to help people learn Spanish, or any other language, in short order. You might hear promises of learning a language in just a couple of weeks. Some of the more outrageous claims state that you can learn a language in just a few hours.

While it is true that the right methodology can help you improve your skills without having to spend weeks, or even months, in a language school, it is also true that it is not realistic to learn a language with just a couple of lessons.

The truth is learning a language does require work and dedication. Mainly, it is a matter of focus. When you have the right materials in hand, and you are focused on what you want to achieve, learning a language does not become an arduous endeavor. In fact, it can be a lot of fun.

That is why this book presents you with 21 short stories about various topics. These topics are intended to be interesting, fun, and informative. This way, you will not only learn Spanish but also pick up on other interesting topics. After all, isn't it great that you can learn a language and also practice with some of your favorite topics?

In this volume, you will find that each chapter contains a story. The story is intended to introduce the topic and present the target vocabulary in such a way that you can navigate through the story in an easy and digestible manner. This book is hardly about complex grammar rules and learning the names of everything in the language. This book is all about getting you off the ground in your effort to master this wonderful language.

Then, you will find a summary of the story in Spanish. This summary is meant to serve as a study guide so that you can synthesize your understanding of the topic in a more concise manner. The summary in English will help you to fixate the main idea and topic in your mind. This is intended to serve as a study guide so that you won't have to guess if your understanding of the story was correct or not.

The multiple-choice questions are intended to help you improve your reading comprehension, vocabulary, and grammar skills. The answers provided at the end of the chapter serve as a means of helping you determine your full comprehension of the story.

The most important thing to keep in mind is that learning a language requires one thing, and that is consistency. So, the more consistent you are in your language-learning endeavors, the easier it will be for you to make progress. While you can still make progress even if you don't devote quite as much time to it, the progress you see won't be quite as a significant.

That being said, whether you can devote 15 minutes of your time or one hour a day, the main thing to keep in mind is to be consistent with the amount of time you can dedicate to this book. This way, you can ensure that you will be making progress, even if it's a little every day.

So, don't wait any longer. Dedicate a small chunk of your time every day, and allot it to the study of this book. You can surely take 10 or 15 minutes of a lunch hour, commute, or even right before bedtime to learn Spanish. Whether you are looking to learn Spanish for fun, for an upcoming trip or to improve your job skills, you will find that it is not only rewarding but also personally satisfying.

Good luck!

Chapter One

First Day of Class — Primer día de clases

Hoy es el **primer** día de clases. **Estoy** súper **emocionada** porque estoy en un **nuevo grado**. **También tengo** una nueva **maestra**. Mi maestra se llama Margarita. Es muy **amable**, pero es **estricta**. Todos mis **compañeros** del año **pasado** están **conmigo**. Somos un grupo muy **unido**. Tenemos muchos años de ser amigos.

Este año, **quiero** hacer **muchas** cosas. Quiero **jugar** en el **equipo** de **basquetbol**. Es mi primer año con el basquetbol. Estoy **segura** de que debo **trabajar** mucho, pero sé que lo **lograré**. Es un sueño ser parte del equipo de basquetbol de mi **escuela**.

Otra **meta** para este **año** es aprender un nuevo **idioma**. Quiero **aprender** francés. Es un idioma muy bonito. Es un poco **difícil**, pero no es tan **complicado** como parece. Miro **algunos videos** en línea y puedo **entender** algunas **palabras**. Creo que no será tan difícil.

Mi otra meta para este año es sacar las **mejores** notas de la **clase**. Quiero ser la mejor **estudiante** de mi **generación**. Por eso estoy decidida a hacer mi mejor **esfuerzo** para lograrlo. Con trabajo y **dedicación** sé que lo voy a lograr.

Tengo muchas metas. Pero también estoy muy motivada para lograrlas. Mis padres me **apoyan**. Con su **ayuda**, todo es más **fácil**. Aunque no siempre es fácil lograr las metas, lo importante es hacer un buen esfuerzo. Estoy preparada para dar mi mejor esfuerzo este año. No voy a **perder** las **oportunidades** que tengo.

Pero, la **diversión** también es importante. Mis amigos y yo nos **gusta** divertirnos. Vamos a **fiestas** los **fines de semana**. Nos gusta ir al **cine**, o hacer **deporte** en el **parque**. Mi actividad favorita es ir al cine a ver los **estrenos** más **recientes**. Esta **semana**, hay una nueva **película** de **terror**. A mis amigos no les gusta las películas de terror, pero a mí me encantan. Solo mi amiga Valentina es **valiente**. Ella sí ve estas películas conmigo. A los chicos les da mucho miedo las películas de terror. ¡Es tan **gracioso**!

Es muy divertido pasar el **tiempo** en el cine, **practicando** deportes o haciendo actividades **libres**. Pero creo que es necesario **enfocarse** en las metas de la vida. Sin metas, es imposible alcanzar el **éxito**. Si no tienes metas, no sabes qué es lo que **realmente** quieres lograr. Por eso es que me siento **segura** de lo que quiero ser en la vida.

Estoy muy emocionada por este nuevo año **escolar**. Quiero lograr todas mis metas. El **próximo** año estaré en mi **último** año de **secundaria**. Luego, me voy a la **universidad**. Es **emocionante** pensar que pronto estaré estudiando una carrera universitaria. Estoy decidida que quiero ser **doctor**. Es una carrera difícil. Pero, con esfuerzo lo voy a lograr. Tengo el apoyo de mis padres y mis amigos. Estoy segura de que lo voy a lograr.

Por ahora, debo **concentrarme** en mis clases. La clase más difícil para mí es **matemáticas**. Entonces, debo concentrarme durante esta clase para comprender los **conceptos**. Siempre estudio mucho para mi clase de matemáticas. La clase de **lenguaje** es fácil para mí al igual que las clases de **ciencias**. Pero mi clase favorita es arte. Me gusta mucho pintar y dibujar. Me gusta expresar mis **habilidades artísticas**.

Ya están todos mis amigos en clase. Vamos a **iniciar** con nuestra primera clase del año. ¡Qué nervios! Ya vamos a iniciar un nuevo año. Estoy segura de que todo saldrá bien. Estoy con mis amigos y tengo todas las ganas para ser exitosa. No puedo **esperar** más. Quiero lograr las mejores notas este año, jugar en el equipo de basquetbol y aprender un nuevo idioma. Yo sé que es **bastante** trabajo, pero con un poco de esfuerzo y dedicación, lo voy a lograr.

Ahora, solo queda iniciar las clases y echarle ganas. Estoy **optimista** sobre el **futuro**. Pronto lograré todas mis metas… al igual que divertirme con mis amigos. Juntos, vamos a tener el mejor año de **nuestras vidas**.

Resumen de la historia

Hoy es el primer día de un nuevo año escolar. Estoy emocionada porque tengo muchas metas. Quiero ser la mejor estudiante de la clase. También quiero aprender un nuevo idioma. Estoy interesada en aprender francés. También quiero jugar en el equipo de basquetbol de mi escuela. Estoy motivada porque estoy segura de que será un buen año. Estoy con todos mis amigos del año pasado. A mis amigos y yo nos gusta divertirnos. Hacemos deporte los fines de semana, vamos al cine y estamos en fiestas. Pero también nos gusta estudiar mucho para sacar buenas notas en los exámenes. Voy a tener el mejor año de mi vida. Pero, debo esforzarme para alcanzar mis metas. Tengo el apoyo de mis padres y de mis amigos. Así que tengo todo lo que necesito para alcanzar mis metas este año. Ya vamos a iniciar con la primera clase. ¡Qué nervios!

Summary of the Story

Today is the first day of the new school year. I am excited because I have many goals. I want to be the best student in class. I also want to learn a new language. I am interested in learning French. I also want to play in my school basketball team. I am motivated because I am sure it will be a good year. I am with all my friends from last year. My friends and I like to have fun. We do sports on weekends, we go to the movies, and we go to parties. But we also like to study hard to get good grades on exams. I will have the best year of my life. But, I must strive to reach my goals.

I have the support of my parents and my friends. So, I have everything I need to reach my goals this year. We are going to start with the first class. How nerve-wracking!

Vocabulary

1. **hoy** today
2. **primer** first
3. **estoy** I am
4. **emocionada** excited
5. **nuevo** new
6. **grado** grade
7. **también** as well
8. **tengo** I have
9. **maestra** teacher
10. **amable** nice
11. **estricta** strict
12. **compañeros** companions
13. **pasado** past
14. **conmigo** with me
15. **unido** united
16. **quiero** I want
17. **muchas** many
18. **jugar** to play
19. **equipo** team
20. **basquetbol** basketball
21. **segura** safe
22. **trabajar** to work
23. **lograré** I will achieve
24. **escuela** school
25. **meta** goal
26. **año** year
27. **idioma** language

28. **aprender** to learn
29. **difícil** hard
30. **complicado** complicated
31. **algunos** some
32. **videos** videos
33. **entender** understand
34. **palabras** words
35. **mejores** top
36. **clase** class
37. **estudiante** student
38. **generación** generation
39. **esfuerzo** effort
40. **dedicación** dedication
41. **apoyan** support
42. **ayuda** help
43. **fácil** easy
44. **perder** to lose
45. **oportunidades** opportunities
46. **diversión** fun
47. **gusta** like
48. **fiestas** parties
49. **fines de semana** weekends
50. **cine** movie theater
51. **deporte** sport
52. **parque** park
53. **estrenos** premieres
54. **recientes** recent
55. **semana** week
56. **película** movie

57. **terror**	terror
58. **valiente**	brave
59. **gracioso**	funny
60.**tiempo**	weather
61. **practicando**	practicing
62. **libres**	free
63. **enfocarse**	focus
64. **éxito**	success
65. **realmente**	really
66. **segura**	safe
67. **escolar**	school
68. **próximo**	next
69. **último**	latest
70. **secundaria**	high school
71. **universidad**	college
72. **emocionante**	exciting
73. **doctor**	doctor
74. **concentrarme**	concentrate
75. **matemáticas**	maths
76. **conceptos**	concepts
77. **lenguaje**	language
78. **ciencias**	sciences
79. **habilidades**	skills
80.**artísticas**	artistic
81. **iniciar**	start
82. **esperar**	wait
83. **bastante**	quite
84. **optimista**	optimistic
85. **futuro**	future

86. **nuestras**	our
87. **vidas**	lives

Questions About the Story

1. ¿Cuál es el nuevo idioma que quiero aprender?
    a. Español
    b. Inglés
    c. Francés
    d. Alemán
2. ¿Cuál es el deporte que quiero jugar en el equipo de mi escuela?
    a. Béisbol
    b. Basquetbol
    c. Volibol
    d. Tenis
3. ¿Cuáles son mis clases favoritas?
    a. Matemáticas y ciencias
    b. Matemáticas e inglés
    c. Lenguaje y arte
    d. Lenguaje y deportes
4. ¿Cuál es la actividad que más me gusta con mis amigos?
    a. Ir al cine
    b. Jugar tenis
    c. Estudiar francés
    d. Ver televisión
5. ¿Cuál es mi meta para este año?
    a. Ser la mejor estudiante de mi generación

b. Tener muchos amigos en mi generación

c. Aprender todos los idiomas de la escuela

d. Practicar todos los deportes que hay

Answers

1. C
2. B
3. A
4. A
5. A

Chapter Two

Traveling Through Latin America -- Viajar por Latinoamérica

Latinoamérica es una **región** muy **amplia**. En **total**, hay **veinte** países en Latinoamérica. Todos los países **tienen** al español como idioma **oficial** con **excepción** de Brasil, cuyo idioma oficial es el **portugués**, y Haití, cuyo idioma oficial es el francés.

Cuando viajas por Latinoamérica, es **común** ver todo **tipo** de **paisajes**, **climas**, **culturas** y **tradiciones**. Muchas de las **tradiciones** son de **origen europeo**, **particularmente** de España, Francia y Portugal, o bien, **ancestrales** de origen **indígena** o **africano**. Esta **mezcla** de tradiciones y culturas hacen de Latinoamérica, una región muy **diversa**.

La **diversidad** también **aplica** a los diferentes tipos de **ecosistemas** que se **encuentran** en la región. Existen ecosistemas **tropicales** como la **selva** en México y Guatemala, o bien, la selva **tropical** de las Amazonas en Brasil, Colombia, Ecuador, Perú y Bolivia. También existen ecosistemas **secos**, tipo **desierto**, como es el caso de Chile y Perú, o bien, ecosistemas **fríos** como la Patagonia en Chile y Argentina. **En definitiva**, **existe** un poco para todos los gustos.

Latinoamérica también es una región **llena** de mucha **historia**. La tradición **española** y **portuguesa** a lo largo de la región se puede ver en los diferentes tipos de **edificios**, **monumentos** e **iglesias** en todos los países de la región. **En algunos casos**, los edificios e iglesias tienen más de **cuatrocientos** años de historia. Pero, cada país tiene su **propia** historia que **contar**. Es por ello que debes visitar cada país para conocer más **acerca** de su historia.

Sin embargo, la historia de Latinoamérica **comienza** hace varios **siglos**. En cada país, existe una **rica** cultura e historia **sobre** pueblos **prehispánicos**, es decir, grupos **sociales** previos a la **venida** de los europeos. Estos grupos de personas mantienen vivas sus costumbres y cultura a través de las diversas tradiciones en **cada** país.

Por ejemplo, en México se celebra el "Día de los Muertos", lo cual es una **fusión** de la **celebración** tradicional con la cultura española. Esta celebración es una de las más **grandes** en toda Latinoamérica. Es **conocida** por sus **colores**, **música** y rica **comida**.

Otra celebración muy conocida es el Carnaval en Brasil. Esta celebración es una **mezcla** de las tradiciones prehispánicas con la cultura europea. El **resultado** es una **fiesta nacional** que **atrae** la **atención** de **todo el mundo**. Visitar Brasil en **época** de Carnaval es una **experiencia singular** para **cualquier turista**. Además, se la música alegra y viva, también se ven los **disfraces** elegantes y elaborados. Estos son la **atracción principal** del Carnaval.

Para los **amantes** de la **arqueología**, existen **templos** y **ruinas** de **civilizaciones anteriores**. Por ejemplo, las ruinas de los antiguos **Mayas ubicados** en el sur de México, Guatemala y Honduras son visitadas por miles de turistas cada año. Las ciudades de Teotihuacán en México, Tikal en Guatemala, y Copán en Honduras, son las principales atracciones. **Vale la pena** realizar un viaje a estas **ciudades** tan **emblemáticas**.

Otro sitio muy **famoso** es Macchu Picchu en Perú. Este es el sitio más conocido del antiguo **Imperio** Inca. Este es un lugar lleno de historia y muchas leyendas. Es un viaje **impresionante** que **jamás** se podrá olvidar. **Miles** de turistas llegan cada año para conocer este lugar tan lleno de **misterio** y **magia**. Además, las fotografías en este **punto** son **únicas**. No hay mejor lugar para **tomarse fotografías inolvidables**.

Estos son **apenas** algunas de las **maravillas** que hay en Latinoamérica. Existen tantos **lugares** como **playas impresionantes**, **montañas majestuosas**, **volcanes activos**, y diversidad **biológica** que no se puede encontrar en **ninguna** otra parte. En definitiva, viajar por Latinoamérica es una oportunidad singular para conocer partes del mundo **inigualables**. Lo mejor de todo es que las personas son amables y amigables. Además, la comida es **deliciosa**. En realidad, no hay más **excusas**. Viajar por Latinoamérica es una experiencia singular.

Resumen de la historia

Latinoamérica es una región diversa en cultura y clima. Existen todo tipo de climas para disfrutar. Hay desde playas impresionantes hasta regiones frías. Hay montañas, volcanes y selvas para conocer. En definitiva, la naturaleza es única.

También existe una diversidad cultural en cada país. La fusión de las cultural prehispánicas con la cultura europea se evidencia en la riqueza de la comida y la belleza de las tradiciones. Cada país está lleno de historia que va desde hace miles de años.

En Latinoamérica se pueden visitar lugares como monumentos, ruinas, edificios e iglesias que tienen hasta cuatrocientos años de historia. Todos estos lugares están llenos de misterio y magia. Existen muchas leyendas acerca de estos lugares.

Pero lo mejor de viajar por Latinoamérica son las personas. Las personas son amigables y siempre están para ayudar a los turistas. Viajar por Latinoamérica es una experiencia única e inolvidable.

Summary of the Story

Latin America is a diverse region in regards to culture and climate. There are all kinds of climates to enjoy. They range from stunning beaches to cold regions. There are mountains, volcanoes, and jungles to know. In short, nature is unique.

There is also cultural diversity in each country. The fusion of pre-Hispanic culture with European culture is evident in the richness of food and the beauty of traditions. Each country is full of history that goes back to thousands of years ago.

In Latin America, you can visit places, such as monuments, ruins, buildings, and churches that have up to four hundred years of history. All of these places are full of mystery and magic. There are many legends about these places.

But the best thing about traveling through Latin America is the people. People are friendly and always there to help tourists. Traveling in Latin America is a unique and unforgettable experience.

Vocabulary

1. **región**	region
2. **amplia**	wide
3. **total**	total
4. **veinte**	twenty
5. **tienen**	they have
6. **oficial**	official
7. **excepción**	exception
8. **portugués**	Portuguese
9. **cuando**	when
10. **común**	common
11. **tipo**	kind
12. **paisajes**	landscapes
13. **climas**	climates
14. **culturas**	cultures
15. **tradiciones**	traditions
16. **origen**	origin
17. **europeo**	European
18. **particularmente**	particularly
19. **ancestrales**	ancestral
20. **indígena**	indigenous
21. **africano**	African
22. **mezcla**	mixture
23. **diversa**	diverse
24. **diversidad**	diversity
25. **aplica**	apply
26. **ecosistemas**	ecosystems
27. **encuentran**	they find

28. **tropicales** tropical

29. **selva** jungle

30. **tropical** tropical

31. **secos** dry

32. **desierto** desert

33. **fríos** cold

34. **en definitiva** definitely

35. **existe** exists

36. **llena** full

37. **historia** history

38. **española** Spanish

39. **portuguesa** Portuguese

40. **edificios** buildings

41. **monumentos** monuments

42. **iglesias** churches

43. **en algunos casos** in some cases

44. **cuatrocientos** four hundred

45. **propia** own

46. **contar** tell

47. **acerca** about

48. **sin embargo** but nevertheless

49. **comienza** begins

50. **siglos** centuries

51. **rica** delicious

52. **sobre** on

53. **prehispánicos** prehispanic

54. **sociales** social

55. **venida** coming

56. **cada** every

57. **por ejemplo**	for example
58. **fusión**	fusion
59. **celebración**	celebration
60. **grandes**	big
61. **conocida**	known
62. **colores**	colors
63. **música**	music
64. **comida**	food
65. **mezcla**	mixture
66. **resultado**	result
67. **fiesta**	party
68. **nacional**	national
69. **atrae**	attracts
70. **atención**	attention
71. **todo el mundo**	all the world
72. **época**	time
73. **experiencia**	experience
74. **singular**	singular
75. **cualquier**	any
76. **turista**	tourist
77. **disfraces**	costumes
78. **atracción**	attraction
79. **principal**	principal
80. **amantes**	lovers
81. **arqueología**	archeology
82. **templos**	temples
83. **ruinas**	ruins
84. **civilizaciones**	civilizations
85. **anteriores**	previous

86. **mayas**	Maya
87. **ubicados**	located
88. **vale la pena**	worth it
89. **ciudades**	cities
90. **emblemáticas**	emblematic
91. **famoso**	famous
92. **imperio**	empire
93. **impresionante**	awesome
94. **jamás**	never
95. **miles**	thousands
96. **misterio**	mystery
97. **magia**	magic
98. **punto**	point
99. **únicas**	unique
100. **tomarse**	be taken
101. **fotografías**	photographs
102. **inolvidables**	unforgettable
103. **apenas**	barely
104. **maravillas**	wonders
105. **lugares**	places
106. **playas**	beaches
107. **impresionantes**	awesome
108. **montañas**	mountains
109. **majestuosas**	majestic
110. **volcanes**	volcanoes
111. **activos**	assets
112. **biológica**	biological
113. **ninguna**	any
114. **inigualables**	unparalleled

115. **deliciosa**	delicious
116. **excusas**	excuses

Questions About the Story

1. ¿Qué lugares puedes encontrar en Latinoamérica?
    a. Centros comerciales
    b. Edificios y monumentos
    c. Aviones y trenes de carga
    d. Muchos lugares lindos
2. ¿Qué son los Mayas y los Incas?
    a. Lugares turísticos
    b. Edificios históricos
    c. Sociedades prehispánicas
    d. Países impresionantes
3. ¿Cómo son las personas en Latinoamérica?
    a. Terribles
    b. Altas
    c. Bonitas
    d. Amables
4. ¿Cuál es el origen de los países Latinoamericanos?
    a. Diverso
    b. Importante
    c. Variado
    d. Europeo
5. ¿Cómo es la experiencia en Latinoamérica?
    a. Grande

b. Espacial

c. Singular

d. Importante

Answers

1. B
2. C
3. D
4. D
5. C

Chapter Three

Buying a New Car -- Comprando un auto nuevo

Para muchas **personas**, **comprar** un **auto** nuevo es un **sueño** hecho **realidad**. Existen personas que pasan mucho tiempo **trabajando** y **ahorrando** su **dinero** para comprar el auto de sus sueños. En algunos casos, estos autos son **costosos**. Por eso es que deben **ahorrar** por mucho tiempo. En otros casos, un **préstamo** por el valor del auto **ayuda** a **comprarlo**. Pero, se debe **pagar** las **cuotas** del auto mes a **mes**. **Entonces**, es **igualmente necesario contar** con dinero para pagar el auto.

Algunas personas sueñan con un auto de **lujo**. Este tipo de auto cuenta con muchas **características especiales** como **asientos** de **cuero**, **equipo electrónico**, **transmisión automática** y un **estéreo** de potente. Estos autos son ideales para la **ciudad** ya que son **cómodos** especialmente cuando hay mucho **tráfico**. Además, estos autos cuentan con **bastante espacio** para para llevar a varias personas.

Otras personas sueñan con un **auto deportivo**. Este tipo de auto es **rápido** y **pequeño**. Cuenta con un **motor** potente que puede alcanzar **velocidades** muy **altas**. Es ideal para **conducirlo** en **autopista** o en **carreteras** libres de **límite** de velocidad. Estos autos **usualmente** son de dos **plazas**, es decir, solamente dos personas pueden ir dentro del auto. También **cuentan** con transmisión automática, o bien **manual**, según la **preferencia** del **conductor**.

También existe un tipo de auto conocido como "**camioneta**". Este tipo de auto sirve para **transportar** personas y su **equipaje** especialmente cuando se hacen **viajes** largos. Estos son autos **grandes**, con un motor **fuerte**, y con mucho espacio. Son muy cómodos y son **útiles** tanto en la ciudad como en carretera libre. Esta clase autos permite una **experiencia** más cómoda sobre todo cuando se hacen viajes largos.

Luego, existe otro tipo de auto conocido como " **pick-up**". Este tipo de auto sirve para trabajo. Usualmente, tiene dos plazas ya que la parte **trasera** está **abierta**. Entonces, la parte trasera sirve para **colocar objetos** de **carga** como **muebles**, **cajas**, **materiales** para el hogar, o cualquier otro objeto grande. Estos autos son muy útiles para personas que **normalmente** cargan cosas de un **lado hacia** otro.

En definitiva, comprar un auto es muy útil para el transporte personal y de la **familia**. Algunas personas usan su auto para ir a su trabajo. Otras personas lo usan para los **fines de semana**. Algunas otras personas usan su auto como **pasatiempo**. Por ejemplo, hay personas que disfrutan las **competencias** de autos.

Pero para las personas que compran y venden autos, esto se **convierte** en un **negocio**. Una **concesionaria** es una **empresa** en donde se **venden** autos de todo tipo. En general, una concesionaria trabaja con una **marca** específica de auto. Aunque hay algunas concesionarias que trabajan todo tipo de autos y de **cualquier** marca. En una empresa de estas, una persona puede encontrar su auto **ideal** y a un **buen precio**.

Las personas también pueden vender su auto de manera **independiente**. Esto se conoce como una **venta privada**. En una venta privada, una persona **decide** vender su auto a una persona interesada en **comprarlo**. Estas dos personas se ponen de acuerdo en el precio, y listo, se vende el auto. Una práctica común en este caso es llevar el auto con un **mecánico**. El mecánico tiene **herramientas** para **revisar** el auto. Con esto, se sabe si el auto está en buenas **condiciones** o si necesita **reparaciones**. Por eso, la opinión de un buen mecánico es importante antes de comprar un **auto usado**.

En general, comprar un auto es un sueño para muchas personas. Lo importante es saber si el auto está en buen **estado** sobre todo si es un auto usado. Entonces, es buena idea **investigar** un auto **previo** a comprarlo. **De lo contrario**, comprar un auto en **mal estado** puede resultar en una **mala experiencia**.

Resumen de la hostoria

Comprar un auto es un sueño para muchas personas. Algunas personas ahorran su dinero mucho tiempo para comprar el auto de sus sueños. Otras personas obtienen un préstamo para comprar el auto que desean.

Existen diferentes tipos de autos. Por ejemplo, existen autos de lujo, deportivos, camionetas y "pick-ups". El tipo de auto que una persona comprar depende del uso. Las personas que viven en la ciudad usualmente compran un auto de lujo. Las personas que disfrutan la velocidad compran un auto deportivo. Las personas que hacen viajes largos compran una camioneta. Las personas que usan un auto para su trabajo pueden comprar un "pick-up".

Siempre es buena idea revisar un auto usado con un mecánico. Si el auto está en buenas condiciones, es una buena compra. Pero si el auto está en malas condiciones, éste podría ser una mala compra. Por eso es importante la opinión de un buen mecánico antes de comprar un auto usado.

Summary of the Story

Buying a car is a dream for many people. Some people save their money for a long time to buy the car of their dreams. Other people get a loan to buy the car they want.

There are different types of cars. For example, there are luxury cars, sports cars, SUVs, and pick-ups. The type of car a person buys depends on the use. People who live in the city usually buy a luxury car. People who enjoy racing buy a sports car. People who make long trips buy an SUV. People who use a car for work can buy a pick-up.

It is always a good idea to check a used car with a mechanic. If the car is in good condition, it is a good purchase. But if the car is in bad condition, this could be a bad purchase. That is why the opinion of a good mechanic is important before buying a used car.

Vocabulary

1. **personas**	people
2. **comprar**	to buy
3. **auto**	car
4. **sueño**	dream
5. **realidad**	reality
6. **trabajando**	working
7. **ahorrando**	saving
8. **dinero**	money
9. **costosos**	expensive
10. **ahorrar**	save money
11. **préstamo**	loan
12. **ayuda**	help
13. **comprarlo**	buy
14. **pagar**	pay
15. **cuotas**	dues
16. **mes**	month
17. **entonces**	so
18. **igualmente**	equally
19. **necesario**	necessary
20. **contar**	tell
21. **lujo**	luxury
22. **características**	characteristics
23. **especiales**	specials
24. **asientos**	seating
25. **cuero**	leather
26. **equipo electrónico**	electronic equipment
27. **transmisión**	transmission

28. **automática**	automatic
29. **estéreo**	stereo
30. **ciudad**	city
31. **cómodos**	comfortable
32. **tráfico**	traffic
33. **bastante**	quite
34. **espacio**	space
35. **auto deportivo**	sports car
36. **rápido**	quick
37. **pequeño**	small
38. **motor**	engine
39. **velocidades**	speeds
40. **altas**	high
41. **conducirlo**	drive it
42. **autopista**	freeway
43. **carreteras**	roads
44. **límite**	limit
45. **usualmente**	usually
46. **plazas**	plazas
47. **cuentan**	they count
48. **manual**	manual
49. **preferencia**	preference
50. **conductor**	driver
51. **camioneta**	van
52. **transportar**	transport
53. **equipaje**	luggage
54. **viajes**	travels
55. **grandes**	big
56. **fuerte**	strong

57. **útiles**	tools
58. **experiencia**	experience
59. **pick-up**	pick-up
60. **trasera**	rear
61. **abierta**	open
62. **colocar**	place
63. **objetos**	objects
64. **carga**	load
65. **muebles**	furniture
66. **cajas**	boxes
67. **materiales**	materials
68. **normalmente**	usually
69. **lado**	side
70. **hacia**	toward
71. **en definitiva**	definitely
72. **familia**	family
73. **fines de semana**	weekends
74. **pasatiempo**	hobby
75. **competencias**	competitions
76. **convierte**	converts
77. **negocio**	deal
78. **concesionaria**	dealership
79. **empresa**	company
80. **venden**	do you sell
81. **marca**	brand
82. **cualquier**	any
83. **ideal**	ideal
84. **buen**	good
85. **precio**	price

86. **independiente**	independent
87. **venta privada**	private sale
88. **decide**	decide
89. **comprarlo**	buy
90. **mecánico**	mechanic
91. **herramientas**	tools
92. **revisar**	check
93. **condiciones**	terms
94. **reparaciones**	repairs
95. **auto usado**	used car
96. **en general**	in general
97. **estado**	state
98. **investigar**	research
99. **previo**	previous
100. **de lo contrario**	on the contrary
101. **mal estado**	disrepair
102. **mala experiencia**	bad experience

Questions About the Story

1. ¿Qué es comprar un auto para muchas personas?
    a. Una idea
    b. Un sueño
    c. Un concepto
    d. Una necesidad
2. ¿Qué necesitas para comprar un auto?
    a. Comida
    b. Trabajo
    c. Dinero
    d. Poder
3. ¿Dónde puedes comprar un auto?
    a. En una tienda
    b. En el centro comercial
    c. En el trabajo
    d. En una concesionaria
4. ¿Cómo puedes comprar un auto?
    a. Con un préstamo
    b. Con tus ideas
    c. Con un tiempo
    d. Con el trabajo
5. ¿Qué hace el mecánico?
    a. Trabaja duro

b. Es un amigo

c. Revisa el auto

d. Hace trabajo

Answers

1. B
2. C
3. D
4. A
5. C

Chapter Four

A Healthy Life — Una vida saludable

Vivir una **vida saludable** es una meta de muchas personas. **A veces**, no es **fácil** vivir **saludablemente**. Tomar las **decisiones correctas** en cuanto a la **alimentación** y la **actividad física** requieren estudio y **comprensión** sobre la mejor **manera** de **alcanzar** las metas personales.

Por ejemplo, existen personas que desean **perder** un poco de **peso**. Estas personas no **desean** verse como **modelos**. **Simplemente** quieren perder peso y **sentirse** mejor. **Para ello**, es importante tener una **dieta** saludable y hacer **ejercicio regular**. Con esta **combinación**, pueden perder peso, **lucir** mejor, y sentirse bien.

Luego, hay otras personas que quieren verse lo mejor posible. Es por ello que tienen una dieta **estricta** y hacen bastante ejercicio, usualmente en el **gimnasio**. Este tipo de personas van **prácticamente** todos los días al gimnasio. Su meta es ser saludables y lucir muy bien.

Para aquellas personas que son **atletas**, su meta es **prepararse** para un deporte **específico**. El deporte particular **no importa**. Lo que importa es que tienen la

preparación necesaria para ser **competitivo** en ese deporte. Esto requiere de mucho tiempo y **esfuerzo**. El resultado es una condición física adecuada para el deporte que desean practicar.

La combinación para una vida saludable es una buena **nutrición** y ejercicio **regular**. **Primeramente**, una buena nutrición se basa en **comer frutas** y **vegetables** más que comidas **procesadas**. Las comidas procesadas son altas en **azúcar** y contienen **químicos**. Estos químicos y azúcar hacen que las personas **suban** de peso. Por lo tanto, es **difícil** perder peso cuando se tiene una dieta basada en comidas procesadas.

Al respecto del azúcar, es buena idea **evitar** consumir azúcar **excesivamente**. Si se consume mucha azúcar, el cuerpo la **guarda** para futuro uso. **Con el tiempo**, se **gana** peso. Lo mismo sucede con los **carbohidratos**. Si se consumen demasiados carbohidratos, también se puede subir de peso.

Pero esto no quiere decir que no **debes** consumir azúcar y carbohidratos. Lo que **significa** es que debes consumir en una **cantidad moderada**. Eso es todo. Si consumes la cantidad **recomendada** por un **médico** o **nutricionista**, estarás perfectamente bien. Estás en una dieta balanceada para tu una vida saludable.

Otro elemento importante de una dieta balanceada es consumir **carnes** en cantidad moderada. Consumir **pollo** y **pescado** es buena idea porque contienen poca **grasa**. La carne de **cerdo** y **res** son buenas, pero en cantidades **menores**. Entonces, debes consumir más pollo y pescado, y menos cerdo y res.

Así mismo, el ejercicio regular es muy bueno para **mantener** un cuerpo saludable. Para hacer ejercicio regular no se necesita estar **horas** y horas en el gimnasio. Ejercicio como **caminar**, **levantar pesas** por **treinta minutos**, o bien, practicar algún deporte como la **natación**, son formas adecuadas para mantener el cuerpo en forma.

Además, el ejercicio regular ayuda a **quemar** grasa y perder peso. Cuando se combina una buena nutrición con ejercicio regular, es **posible** alcanzar el peso **ideal** al igual que estar **sano**. Lo importante es mantener un buen **balance** entre la nutrición y el deporte.

Finalmente, el otro **elemento esencial** para una vida saludable es **dormir adecuadamente**. Cuando una persona duerme adecuadamente, su cuerpo se recupera del **desgaste diario**. Dormir **ocho** horas diarias es lo recomendado por los doctores. Cuando se duerme menos de ocho horas diarias, el cuerpo **sufre** de cambios negativos. Por eso es importante dormir la cantidad de horas recomendadas.

Todos estos **consejos** son útiles para vivir una vida saludable. Cuando se combinan estos consejos, es posible alcanzar el peso ideal, la figura deseada y el nivel de energía necesario para el trabajo diario. Si se mantiene una **actitud positiva**, todos estos elementos hacen de un cuerpo saludable.

Resumen de la historia

La combinación de una dieta balanceada y ejercicio regular es la mejor manera para lograr un cuerpo ideal y una vida saludable. Cuando una persona consume mucha azúcar y carbohidratos, al igual que comida procesada, puede subir de peso. Por eso es importante consumir azúcar y carbohidratos moderadamente. Así mismo, es esencial evitar muchas comidas procesadas.

Una buena nutrición basada en frutas y vegetales es ideal para mantener un buen peso. Así mismo, el ejercicio regular consiste en caminar, levantar pesas o practicar algún deporte como la natación. El ejercicio es importante para ayudar a bajar de peso y alcanzar la figura deseada. No se necesita hacer mucho ejercicio. Treinta minutos al día es un buen comienzo.

También es importante dormir la cantidad recomendada por los doctores. Usualmente, ocho horas es suficiente para sentirse bien y recuperarse de un día lleno de actividades. Si se duerme menos de ocho horas por mucho tiempo, el cuerpo puede empezar a tener problemas de salud. Con estos consejos, es posible alcanzar una vida saludable y estar en forma.

Summary of the Story

The combination of a balanced diet and regular exercise is the best way to achieve an ideal body and a healthy life. When a person consumes a lot of sugar and carbohydrates, such as in processed food, they can gain weight. That is why it is important to consume sugar and carbohydrates moderately. Likewise, it is essential to avoid many processed foods.

Good nutrition based on fruits and vegetables is ideal for maintaining a good weight. Also, a regular exercise consists of walking, lifting weights, or playing sports such as swimming. Exercise is important in losing weight and achieving one's desired figure. You do not need to exercise much. Thirty minutes a day is a good start.

It is also important to get the number of hours of sleep recommended by doctors. Usually, eight hours is enough to feel good and recover from a day full of activities. If you sleep less than eight hours for a long time, the body may begin to have health problems. With these tips, it is possible to achieve a healthy life and be fit.

Vocabulary

1. **vivir**	live
2. **vida**	lifetime
3. **saludable**	healthy
4. **a veces**	sometimes
5. **fácil**	easy
6. **saludablemente**	healthily
7. **decisiones**	decisions
8. **correctas**	correct
9. **alimentación**	feeding
10. **actividad física**	physical activity
11. **comprensión**	understanding
12. **manera**	way
13. **alcanzar**	reach
14. **perder**	to lose
15. **peso**	weight
16. **desean**	wish
17. **modelos**	models
18. **simplemente**	simply
19. **sentirse**	feel
20. **para ello**	for it
21. **dieta**	diet
22. **ejercicio regular**	regular exercise
23. **combinación**	combination
24. **lucir**	show off
25. **luego**	then
26. **estricta**	strict
27. **gimnasio**	fitness center

28. **prácticamente** practically
29. **atletas** athletes
30. **prepararse** get prepared
31. **específico** specific
32. **no importa** no matter
33. **preparación** preparation
34. **necesaria** necessary
35. **competitivo** competitive
36. **esfuerzo** effort
37. **nutrición** nutrition
38. **regular** regular
39. **primeramente** firstly
40. **comer** eat
41. **frutas** fruits
42. **vegetables** vegetables
43. **procesadas** processed
44. **azúcar** sugar
45. **químicos** chemists
46. **suban** go up
47. **difícil** hard
48. **al respecto** about
49. **evitar** avoid
50. **excesivamente** excessively
51. **guarda** guard
52. **con el tiempo** over time
53. **gana** win
54. **carbohidratos** carbohydrates
55. **debes** you must
56. **significa** it means

57. **cantidad** quantity

58. **moderada** moderate

59. **recomendada** recommended

60. **médico** doctor

61. **nutricionista** nutritionist

62. **carnes** meats

63. **pollo** chicken

64. **pescado** fish

65. **grasa** grease

66. **cerdo** pork

67. **res** beef

68. **menores** minors

69. **así mismo** likewise

70. **mantener** keep

71. **horas** hours

72. **caminar** walk

73. **levantar pesas** weightlifting

74. **treinta** thirty

75. **minutos** minutes

76. **natación** swimming

77. **quemar** burn

78. **posible** possible

79. **ideal** ideal

80. **sano** healthy

81. **balance** balance

82. **finalmente** finally

83. **elemento** element

84. **esencial** essential

85. **dormir** sleep

86. **adecuadamente** adequately

87. **desgaste** wear

88.**diario** daily

89. **ocho** eight

90.**sufre** suffers

91. **consejos** tips

92. **actitud** attitude

93. **positiva** positive

Questions About the Story

1. ¿Cuáles son los elementos para una vida saludable?
    a. Una buena nutrición
    b. Muchas horas de ejercicio
    c. Mucha comida saludable
    d. Un poco de buena suerte
2. ¿Cuáles son las comidas que debes evitar?
    a. Comidas con vegetables
    b. Comidas procesadas
    c. Comidas con aceite
    d. Comidas con café
3. ¿Dónde puedes hacer ejercicio?
    a. En el trabajo
    b. En el aire
    c. En el gimnasio
    d. En el autobús
4. ¿Cuántas horas debes dormir?
    a. Cinco
    b. Seis
    c. Siete
    d. Ocho
5. ¿Qué pasa si no duermes bien?
    a. Tu cuerpo crece

b. Tu cuerpo vive

c. Tu cuerpo sufre

d. Tu cuerpo habla

Answers

1. A
2. B
3. C
4. D
5. C

Chapter Five

A New House — Una casa nueva

Hoy nos **estamos mudando** a una **casa** nueva. Esta casa es **increíble**. Es mucho **más grande** que mi casa **anterior**. Esta casa tiene **todo** lo que yo quiero. Es un sueño hecho realidad. Cada parte de la casa es **alucinante**. No **puedo** creer que voy a vivir **aquí**. Voy a **describir** lo increíble que es esta casa.

Primero, la casa tiene **cuatro habitaciones**. Cada habitación tiene su **propio cuarto** de **baño**. Es **genial** porque hay **privacidad** en cada habitación. Entonces, no hay necesidad de **molestar** a **nadie más**. Se puede hacer uso de cada baño, y **listo**. Las habitaciones son grandes. Hay **suficiente espacio** para una **cama tamaño** king. También tienen un **clóset** en cada uno. Con eso, es posible **guardar ropa**, **zapatos** y otros **artículos personales**. La habitación **principal** tiene un pequeño **balcón**.

Luego, la **sala familiar** está de lujo. Tiene un espacio para una **televisión** grande, **equipo de sonido** y una **consola de video juegos**. Lo mejor de todo es que hay espacio para **sillones** cómodos. Con un sillón de estos, se disfrutan las **películas** y **series de televisión**. También hay una **mesa de centro**. La mesa es ideal para poner cosas, o bien, colocar **tazas**, **platos** y cualquier otro tipo de **alimento**.

El **comedor** está **maravilloso**. La mesa es grande. Es para ocho personas. Es ideal para una **reunión** en familia, o con amigos. Las comidas familiares son muy cómodas con esta mesa. Las sillas son muy bonitas. Creo que es la mejor mesa de todo el mundo.

La **cocina** es **moderna**. Tiene todos los **aparatos** necesarios: una **estufa**, el **refrigerador**, el **fregadero**, un **lavavajillas**, un **horno**, una **cafetera** y un **microondas**. Todas estas comodidades son importantes para la cocina. Yo disfruto cocinar. Es por ello que la cocina me parece **genial**. Creo que mi **próximo proyecto culinario** será un **pastel**. A mi familia le encanta comer los pasteles que hago.

El **garaje** es muy amplio. Hay suficiente espacio para dos autos. No **podemos pedir** más. **Además**, hay un poco de espacio para guardar cosas como **cajas**, **botes** de pintura y **herramientas**. Esto es muy importante puesto que no hay mucho espacio para ese tipo de cosas **dentro** de la casa.

Así mismo, hay un pequeño **cuarto de estudio**. Este cuarto sirve para una **oficina**, o bien, un cuarto en donde los niños pueden **jugar** y hacer sus **tareas** de la escuela. Es ideal para este tipo de actividades. Es un espacio **independiente** que sirve para **concentración**.

Pero **quizá** el mejor lugar de la casa es el **patio trasero**. Este patio es **impresionante**. ¡Es tan grande! Tiene un **árbol** grande. Este árbol da **sombra** cuando hay mucho **sol**, y también da **frutas**. Es un árbol de **manzanas**. Este patio tiene suficiente espacio para una buena **fiesta**. Se puede hacer una **barbacoa** con amigos, **vecinos** y familiares. Lo mejor de todo es que hay espacio para **relajarse**, jugar un poco, o simplemente **descansar** bajo la sombra del árbol. El **césped** es tan suave que **parece** una **alfombra**.

Amo esta casa. Tiene todas las cosas que yo quiero. Es una casa grande, pero **sencilla**. No se tienen muchas cosas **complicadas** como luces **inteligentes** o **paneles solares**. Es una casa simple, como las de siempre. Me siento muy cómoda dentro de esta casa. Creo que podemos vivir en esta casa por muchos años. Hasta el momento, no **encuentro** algo **malo** con esta casa. Todo **me parece** genial.

Y tú, ¿cómo es tu casa? ¿Es grande o es pequeña? ¿**Cuántas** habitaciones tiene? O, ¿vives en un **departamento** en un **edificio**? Los departamentos también son muy **bonitos**. Aunque son más pequeños que una casa, pero no importa. Si tiene todo lo que quieres, entonces, está genial.

Resumen de la historia

Nos estamos mudando a una nueva casa. Esta casa es genial porque tiene todas las cosas que quiero en una casa. Tiene habitaciones grandes, una cocina moderna, una sala familiar genial y un comedor muy cómodo. Creo que esta es la mejor casa del mundo.

Hay cuatro habitaciones. Cada habitación es grande y tiene su propio cuarto de baño. Esto es importante ya que no se molesta a las demás personas. El clóset es perfecto para todas las cosas personales.

Luego, la cocina es moderna. Todos los aparatos son necesarios para cocinar comida deliciosa. Así mismo, el comedor tiene una mesa grande. Esta mesa es ideal para una comida en familia o una reunión con amigos y familia.

La sala familia es genial porque hay espacio para una televisión grande y espacio para sillones cómodos. Creo que esta es una sala familiar impresionante. El garaje es amplio. Hay suficiente espacio para dos autos. También hay espacio para guardar cosas.

Pero, el mejor lugar de todos es el patio trasero. Es muy grande. Es ideal para hacer una barbacoa y pasar tiempo con vecinos, amigos y familia. También hay un árbol grande. Este árbol es perfecto para descansar bajo su sombra.

Summary of the Story

We are moving to a new house. This house is great because it has all the things I want in a house. It has large rooms, a modern kitchen, a great family room, and a very comfortable dining room. I think this is the best house in the world.

There are four rooms. Each room is large and has its own bathroom. This is important since it does not bother other people. The closet is perfect for all personal things.

Then the kitchen is modern. All appliances are necessary to cook delicious food. Also, the dining room has a large table. This table is ideal for a family meal or a meeting with friends and family.

The family room is great because there is room for a large television and space for comfortable chairs. I think this is an impressive family room. The garage is spacious. There is enough space for two cars. There is also space to store things.

But, the best place of all is the backyard. It is very large. It is ideal for making a barbecue and spending time with neighbors, friends, and family. There is also a big tree. This tree is perfect for resting under its shade.

Vocabulary

1. **estamos** we're
2. **mudando** moving
3. **casa** home
4. **increíble** incredible
5. **más** plus
6. **grande** big
7. **anterior** previous
8. **todo** all
9. **alucinante** incredible
10. **puedo** I can
11. **aquí** here
12. **describir** describe
13. **primero** first
14. **cuatro** four
15. **habitaciones** bedrooms
16. **propio** own
17. **cuarto** quarter
18. **baño** bathroom
19. **genial** cool
20. **privacidad** privacy
21. **molestar** bother
22. **nadie más** nobody else
23. **listo** ready
24. **suficiente** enough
25. **espacio** space
26. **cama** bed
27. **tamaño** size

28. **clóset**	closet
29. **guardar**	save
30. **ropa**	clothing
31. **zapatos**	shoes
32. **artículos**	articles
33. **personales**	personal
34. **principal**	principal
35. **balcón**	balcony
36. **sala familiar**	family room
37. **televisión**	TV
38. **equipo de sonido**	stereo
39. **consola de video juegos**	video game console
40. **sillones**	armchairs
41. **películas**	films
42. **series de televisión**	TV series
43. **mesa de centro**	center table
44. **tazas**	cups
45. **platos**	dishes
46. **alimento**	food
47. **comedor**	dining room
48. **maravilloso**	wonderful
49. **reunión**	meeting
50. **cocina**	kitchen
51. **moderna**	modern
52. **aparatos**	gadgets
53. **estufa**	stove
54. **refrigerador**	fridge
55. **fregadero**	sink
56. **lavavajillas**	dishwasher

57. **horno**	oven
58. **cafetera**	coffee maker
59. **microondas**	microwave oven
60. **genial**	cool
61. **próximo**	next
62. **proyecto**	draft
63. **culinario**	culinary
64. **pastel**	cake
65. **garaje**	garage
66. **podemos**	we can
67. **pedir**	ask
68. **además**	further
69. **cajas**	boxes
70. **botes**	boats
71. **herramientas**	tools
72. **dentro**	inside
73. **así mismo**	likewise
74. **cuarto de estudio**	studying room
75. **oficina**	office
76. **jugar**	to play
77. **tareas**	chores
78. **independiente**	independent
79. **concentración**	concentration
80. **quizá**	maybe
81. **patio trasero**	backyard
82. **impresionante**	awesome
83. **árbol**	tree
84. **sombra**	shadow

85. **sol** sun

86. **frutas** fruits

87. **manzanas** apples

88. **fiesta** party

89. **barbacoa** barbecue

90. **vecinos** neighbors

91. **relajarse** relax

92. **descansar** rest

93. **césped** grass

94. **parece** it seems

95. **alfombra** carpet

96. **amo** love

97. **sencilla** simple

98. **complicadas** complicated

99. **inteligentes** smart

100. **paneles solares** solar panels

101. **encuentro** meeting

102. **malo** bad

103. **me parece** it seems to me

104. **cuántas** how many

105. **departamento** apartment

106. **edificio** building

107. **bonitos** pretty

Questions About the Story

1. ¿Cómo son las habitaciones?
    a. Grandes yextrañas
    b. Grandes yterribles
    c. Grandes y cómodas
    d. Grandes y divertidas
2. ¿Cuántas habitaciones tiene la casa?
    a. Tres
    b. Cuatro
    c. Cinco
    d. Seis
3. ¿Qué hay en la sala familiar?
    a. Televisión, sillón y mesa de centro
    b. Mesa de centro, estufa y fregadero
    c. Televisión y equipo de trabajo
    d. Equipo de sonido y microondas
4. ¿Cómo es la cocina?
    a. Moderna
    b. Interesante
    c. Divertida
    d. Curiosamente
5. ¿Cuál es la mejor parte de la casa?
    a. La barbacoa

b. Los vecinos

c. La comida

d. El patio trasero

Answers

1. C
2. B
3. A
4. A
5. D

Chapter Six

Learning a New Language — Aprender un nuevo idioma

Los **idiomas** son **fascinantes**. Un idioma es una **puerta** para un **mundo** nuevo, **lleno** de nuevas **ideas**, **conocimientos** e **información**. **Muchas veces**, una persona no se **imagina** la **cantidad** de cosas nuevas que puede **conocer cuando** aprende un nuevo.

Pero, el **proceso** de aprender un idioma nuevo no es fácil. **De hecho**, aprender un idioma nuevo **requiere** de **esfuerzo** y **constancia**. Todos los idiomas tienen un **grado** de **dificultad**. Por eso es necesario **dedicar** tiempo y trabajo para **desarrollar** una nueva **habilidad** en un idioma nuevo.

El idioma que más personas **estudian** en el mundo es el **inglés**. El inglés es prácticamente el idioma **universal**. Si **varias** personas de diferentes paises del mundo se **reúnen**, es muy **probable** que el idioma de **comunicación** es el inglés. En definitiva, muchas personas se esfuerzan por aprender este idioma.

Pero, el español también es un idioma importante en el mundo. Existen **millones** de personas que hablan el español como **lengua nativa**. También existen millones de personas que lo hablan como **segundo** o **tercer** idioma. Esto hace del español un idioma muy **popular** en el mundo.

Pero, ¿qué puede **hacer** una persona para **mejorar** sus habilidades en idioma español?

Hay muchas **cosas** que una persona puede hacer para mejorar su **nivel** de español.

Lo **primero** que se puede hacer para mejorar el español es **practicar**. **Suena** fácil, pero a veces no **hay** con **quien** practicar. Por eso, es importante hacer amigos que hablan español. Con amigos **hispanoparlantes**, es fácil poner en práctica los **conocimientos** que tienes sobre este **lindo** idioma. Además, practicar con amigos **hispanos** es una buena **actividad** ya que los hispanos son personas muy **cordiales** y amables.

Otra de las actividades que se puede **realizar** es **escuchar música**. Al escuchar música en español, se puede practicar **vocabulario** y **gramática**. La música hispana tiene diferentes **géneros** y **ritmos**. Es por ello que se puede utilizar para practicar todo **tipo** de vocabulario. Cuando se escucha una **canción**, es buena idea

anotar palabras nuevas en un **cuaderno**. Así, es fácil **recordar** las nuevas **palabras** y **frases contenidas** en las canciones.

Una de las mejores actividades para practicar español es con las **telenovelas**. Las telenovelas son **dramas** en donde se desarrolla una **historia** sobre los **personajes principales**. Las novelas, **por lo regular**, son **dramáticas**. Pero también hay novelas **cómicas** y algunas históricas. Lo mejor de todo es que no usan vocabulario **complicado** ni lenguaje muy **avanzado**. Esto facilita practicar el español.

Finalmente, uno de los ejercicios más efectivos para mejorar el nivel de español es **viajar**. Claro, viajar requiere dinero. Pero cuando es posible, viajar a un país de habla hispana es ideal para practicar el español. Cada país de **América Latina** tiene su **propia** forma de **hablar** el español. Entonces dependiendo del país, así es el **acento** y algunos de los **modismos**. Pero, en definitiva, **vale la pena** viajar y conocer más acerca de la **cultura** y de la **riqueza** de cada país.

Viajar es no sólo **divertido**, sino que es una experiencia única y **enriquecedora**. Entre más se viaja, mejor se comprende la cultura, el idioma y las **costumbres**. No se puede perder la **oportunidad** de viajar y practicar el español en los países donde se habla.

En conclusión, existen muchas actividades para mejorar el nivel de español. Pero definitivamente, la mejor manera de mejorar el nivel de español es viajando a cualquier de los **impresionantes** países de América Latina. Esta es una experiencia que **jamás** se **olvidará**. Vale la pena **aprovechar** la oportunidad para conocer más de cerca las **maravillas** de cada país hispano.

Resumen de la historia

El idioma español es uno de los idiomas más populares en el mundo. Hay millones de personas que hablan el español como idioma nativo en el mundo. También hay millones más que lo hablan como segundo o tercer idioma.

Aprender un nuevo idioma no es fácil. Es una actividad que requiere de tiempo y esfuerzo. Muchas veces, requiere de mucho tiempo. Pero con estos consejos, aprender español es más fácil y divertido.

Primero, practicar con amigos hispanoparlantes es una buena idea. Practicar con personas nativas de un idioma es lo mejor para mejorar el nivel. Escuchar música en español es otro de los mejores ejercicios que se puede practicar. La música es una buena manera de aprender nuevo vocabulario.

Luego, las telenovelas también son un buen ejercicio. Con este tipo de programas de televisión, se puede practicar el español de una manera efectiva. Pero la mejor manera de mejorar el nivel de español es viajando a alguno de los países de América Latina. En definitiva, viajar es una de las mejores experiencias en la vida. Dependiendo del país que se visite, se puede aprender mucho acerca de las costumbres y cultura de ese país.

Summary of the Story

The Spanish language is one of the most popular languages in the world. There are millions of people who speak Spanish as a native language. There are also millions more who speak it as a second or third language.

Learning a new language is not easy. It is an activity that requires time and effort. Many times, it takes a lot of time. But with these tips, learning Spanish is easier and more fun.

First, practicing with Spanish-speaking friends is a good idea. Practicing with native people of a language is the best way to improve the level in that language. Listening to music in Spanish is also one of the best exercises that can be practiced. Music is a good way to learn new vocabulary.

Then, watching soap operas is also good exercise. With this type of television program, you can practice Spanish in an effective way. But the best way to improve the level of Spanish is to travel to one of the Latin American countries. In short, traveling is one of the best experiences in life. Depending on the country you visit, you can learn a lot about the customs and culture of that country.

Vocabulary

1. **idiomas** languages
2. **fascinantes** fascinating
3. **puerta** door
4. **mundo** world
5. **lleno** full
6. **ideas** ideas
7. **conocimientos** knowledge
8. **información** information
9. **muchas veces** many times
10. **imagina** imagine
11. **cantidad** quantity
12. **conocer** know
13. **cuando** when
14. **proceso** process
15. **de hecho** in fact
16. **requiere** requires
17. **esfuerzo** effort
18. **constancia** constancy
19. **grado** grade
20. **dificultad** difficulty
21. **dedicar** to dedicate
22. **desarrollar** develop
23. **habilidad** ability
24. **estudian** they study
25. **inglés** English
26. **universal** universal
27. **varias** several

28. **reúnen**	gather
29. **probable**	probable
30. **comunicación**	communication
31. **millones**	millions
32. **lengua nativa**	native language
33. **segundo**	second
34. **tercer**	third
35. **popular**	popular
36. **hacer**	do
37. **mejorar**	to get better
38. **cosas**	things
39. **nivel**	level
40. **primero**	first
41. **practicar**	to practice
42. **suena**	it sounds
43. **hay**	there are
44. **quien**	who
45. **hispanoparlantes**	Spanish speakers
46. **conocimientos**	knowledge
47. **lindo**	cute
48. **hispanos**	Hispanic
49. **actividad**	activity
50. **cordiales**	cordial
51. **realizar**	perform
52. **escuchar**	hear
53. **música**	music
54. **vocabulario**	vocabulary
55. **gramática**	grammar
56. **géneros**	genders

57. **ritmos**	rhythms
58. **tipo**	kind
59. **canción**	song
60.**anotar**	annotate
61. **cuaderno**	notebook
62. **recordar**	remember
63. **palabras**	words
64. **frases**	phrases
65. **contenidas**	contained
66. **telenovelas**	tv soaps
67. **dramas**	dramas
68. **historia**	history
69. **personajes**	characters
70. **principales**	main
71. **por lo regular**	normally
72. **dramáticas**	dramatic
73. **cómicas**	comics
74. **complicado**	complicated
75. **avanzado**	advanced
76. **viajar**	travel
77. **américa latina**	Latin America
78. **propia**	own
79. **hablar**	talk
80.**acento**	accent
81. **modismos**	idioms
82. **vale la pena**	worth it
83. **cultura**	culture
84. **riqueza**	wealth
85. **divertido**	funny

86. **enriquecedora**	enriching
87. **costumbres**	custom
88.**oportunidad**	opportunity
89. **en conclusión**	in conclusion
90.**impresionantes**	awesome
91. **jamás**	never
92. **olvidará**	will forget
93. **aprovechar**	to take advantage of
94. **maravillas**	wonders

Questions About the Story

1. ¿Cuántas personas hablan el español?
   a. Miles de personas
   b. Cientos de personas
   c. Millones de personas
   d. Billones de personas
2. ¿Qué se necesita para aprender un nuevo idioma?
   a. Esfuerzo
   b. Suerte
   c. Dinero
   d. Habilidad
3. ¿Cuál es un buen ejercicio para practicar español?
   a. Ir de viaje
   b. Participar en clase
   c. Escuchar música
   d. Nuevo vocabulario
4. ¿Qué es una telenovela?
   a. Un nuevo libro
   b. Una estación
   c. Una nueva idea
   d. Un programa de televisión
5. ¿Qué puedes aprender de un nuevo país?
   a. Nuevas ideas

b. Nuevos conceptos

c. Sus trabajos

d. Su cultura

Answers

1. C
2. A
3. C
4. D
5. D

Chapter Seven

Pets Are the Ideal Company — Las mascotas son la compañía ideal

Una **mascota** es mucho más que un **animalito** de **compañía**. Una mascota es un amigo **incondicional**. Dependiendo del **tipo** de mascota, la **relación** que una persona tiene con su mascota **cambia**. Por ejemplo, si tienes un **perro**, tu relación con tu perro **será** muy diferente en **comparación** con un **gato**. Pero lo que sí es **cierto**, es que todas las mascotas son la compañía **ideal**.

Los perros son mascotas muy populares. Muchas familias tienen un perro en su **hogar**. Los perros son **altamente** inteligentes, **leales** y **serviciales**. Son animalitos que siempre están al **pendiente** de su **amo**. También son una **excelente** compañía para personas que **viven solas**. Los perros son de **gran utilidad** para personas **no videntes**. Este tipo de perro no es una mascota, sino que es una **guía**.

Los gatos también son mascotas muy populares. Los gatos son animalitos muy **independientes** que **necesitan** su **propio** espacio. Los gatos son tan inteligentes como los perros. Son muy **sensibles** y son una buena compañía en cualquier **momento**. Aunque los gatos no son tan **cariñosos** como los perros. Son animalitos leales que siempre buscan a su amo.

Pero, las mascotas no se **limitan** a los perros y gatos. Existen una diversidad de animalitos que las personas tienen como mascotas. Algunos animalitos, como las **aves**, son mascotas más **tradicionales**. Pero, hay otro tipo de animales, como las **serpientes** y **arañas**, que **algunas** personas tienen como mascotas. Este tipo de mascotas se les conoce como "**mascotas exóticas**".

Si te gustan las mascotas exóticas, entonces aquí hay algunas **sugerencias**.

Si eres **amante** de los **reptiles**, las serpientes son una de las mascotas más populares. Las serpientes no son animales con las cuales se puede jugar. Este tipo de animal se debe mantener en una **jaula**, especialmente si es **venenosa**. Otros tipos de reptiles incluye la **iguana**, la **tortuga** y la **lagartija**.

Luego, las arañas son otro tipo de mascota exótica. Las arañas no se pueden dejar **libres**. Al igual que las serpientes, las arañas se deben guardar en una jaula. Las **tarántulas** son de las mascotas más exóticas.

Además, los **ratones** también son mascotas exóticas. Los **ratones blancos** son relativamente populares entre muchas personas. Pero no son tan comunes como los perros o los gatos. Otros tipos de **roedores** como los **conejillos de india** y los **hámstere**s son animalitos bastante **comunes**.

Hay otras personas que son amantes de los **peces tropicales**. Estos peces son muy **delicados** y necesitan de mucho cuidado. Son muy **caros** y requieren de mucha **atención**. Las personas que tienen peces tropicales **a menudo gastan** mucho dinero en el cuidado de estas mascotas.

En general, el cuidado de una mascota requiere alimentación y un lugar donde dormir. Hay animales que necesitan una **jaula de metal**, o de **vidrio** para vivir. Los animales que requieren de **agua**, como los peces, tortugas y ranas, también necesitan de un espacio especial para vivir.

Cuando una mascota está **enferma**, también es necesario darle atención. Para ello, se lleva con un **veterinario**. Un veterinario es un doctor de animales. Este doctor se **especializa** en cuidar todo tipo de animales, como **vacas**, **caballos**, **pollos** y **cerdos**. Pero hay veterinarios especializados en mascotas.

Si tienes una mascota, **seguramente** entiendes lo especiales que son. Las mascotas son la mejor compañía en la vida. Si no tienes una mascota, puedes investigar los diferentes tipos de mascotas que hay en el mundo. Es seguro que encontrarás un animalito para ti. Es seguro que pronto será tu mejor amigo. Pronto verás que las mascotas son la compañía ideal.

Resumen de la historia

Las mascotas son mucho más que un simple animal de compañía. Las mascotas sirven de compañía, pero también son amigos y hasta guías para personas no videntes. En definitiva, una mascota es una buena compañía para una persona o una familia.

Existen todo tipo de mascotas. Las más comunes son los perros y los gatos. Pero también existen una gran variedad de animalitos que son mascotas. Las mascotas poco comunes se les conoce como "mascotas exóticas". Algunos ejemplos de mascotas exóticas son las serpientes, las arañas y los peces tropicales. Otro tipo de mascotas exóticas son las tortugas y los ratones.

Las mascotas requieren de atención y cuidado. Es importante darles su comida al igual que darles un lugar donde dormir. En algunos casos, se necesita una jaula de metal o de vidrio. En otros casos, se necesita agua para los animalitos. Por ejemplo, los peces tropicales necesitan mucha agua.

Cuando una mascota se enferma, se le debe dar atención. El doctor especializado en mascotas es el veterinario. Este tipo de doctor está entrenado para atender todo tipo de animales. Pero, los veterinarios especializados en mascotas son muy importantes. Estos doctores le dan el cuidado necesario a una mascota enferma.

Summary of the Story

Pets are much more than just a company. Pets serve as companions, but they are also friends and even guides for visually impaired people. In short, a pet is a good company for a person or a family.

There are all kinds of pets. The most common pets are dogs and cats. But there are also a variety of animals that are pets. Uncommon pets are known as "exotic pets." Some examples of exotic pets are snakes, spiders, and tropical fish. Other types of exotic pets are turtles and mice.

Pets require attention and care. It is important to give them their food, as well as a place to sleep. In some cases, a metal or glass cage is needed. In other cases, water is needed for the animals. For example, tropical fish need a lot ofwater.

When a pet gets sick, it should be given attention. The doctor who specializes in pets is a veterinarian. This type of doctor is trained to deal with all kinds of animals. But, veterinarians specializing in pets are very important. These doctors give the necessary care to a sick pet.

Vocabulary

1. **mascota**	pet
2. **animalito**	little animal
3. **compañía**	company
4. **incondicional**	unconditional
5. **tipo**	kind
6. **relación**	relationship
7. **cambia**	change
8. **perro**	dog
9. **será**	will be
10. **comparación**	comparison
11. **gato**	cat
12. **cierto**	true
13. **ideal**	ideal
14. **hogar**	home
15. **altamente**	highly
16. **leales**	loyal
17. **serviciales**	helpful
18. **pendiente**	pending
19. **amo**	love
20. **excelente**	excellent
21. **viven**	they live
22. **solas**	alone
23. **gran**	great
24. **utilidad**	utility
25. **no videntes**	not seeing
26. **guía**	guide
27. **independientes**	independent

28. **necesitan**	they need
29. **propio**	own
30. **sensibles**	sensitive
31. **momento**	moment
32. **cariñosos**	affectionate
33. **limitan**	limit
34. **aves**	birds
35. **tradicionales**	traditional
36. **serpientes**	snakes
37. **arañas**	spiders
38. **algunas**	some
39. **mascotas exóticas**	exotic pets
40. **sugerencias**	suggestions
41. **amante**	lover
42. **reptiles**	reptiles
43. **jaula**	cage
44. **venenosa**	poisonous
45. **iguana**	iguana
46. **tortuga**	turtle
47. **lagartija**	lizard
48. **libres**	free
49. **tarántulas**	tarantulas
50. **ratones**	mice
51. **ratones blancos**	white mice
52. **roedores**	rodents
53. **conejillos de india**	guinea pigs
54. **hámsteres**	hamsters
55. **comunes**	common
56. **peces tropicales**	tropical fish

57. **delicados**	delicate
58. **caros**	expensive
59. **atención**	attention
60.**a menudo**	often
61. **gastan**	they spend
62.**jaula de metal**	metal cage
63. **vidrio**	glass
64. **agua**	water
65. **enferma**	sick
66. **veterinario**	vet
67. **especializa**	specialize
68. **vacas**	cows
69. **caballos**	horses
70. **pollos**	chickens
71. **cerdos**	pigs
72. **seguramente**	surely

Questions About the Story

1. ¿Cuáles son las mascotas más comunes?
    a. Perros y lobos
    b. Perros y gatos
    c. Perros y peces
    d. Perros y animales
2. ¿Cómo son los perros?
    a. Son rápidos
    b. Son interesantes
    c. Son leales
    d. Son nuevos
3. ¿Cómo son los gatos?
    a. Son independientes
    b. Son interesantes
    c. Son difíciles
    d. Son artículos
4. ¿Qué son las mascotas exóticas?
    a. Son mascotas nuevas
    b. Son mascotas interesantes
    c. Son mascotas divertidas
    d. Son mascotas poco comunes
5. ¿Cuáles son las mascotas exóticas?
    a. Las aves

b. Los cerdos

c. Las arañas

d. Las vacas

Answers

1. B
2. C
3. A
4. D
5. C

Chapter Eight

Going Shopping on the Weekend — Salir de compras en el fin de semana

Una de mis actividades **favoritas** es **salir de compras** los fines de semana con mis amigas. Mi lugar **preferido** para ir de compras es el **centro comercial**. Hay un centro comercial **enorme cerca** de mi casa. **Ahí**, se encuentra todo tipo de **tiendas**; desde **ropa** y **zapatos** hasta autos nuevos. Definitivamente tiene de todo.

Mis amigas y yo **disfrutamos** ir de compras **especialmente** cuando hay **ofertas** especiales. Cuando hay ofertas, se puede conseguir buenos **artículos** a buen **precio**. También hay cosas muy **bonitas** a precio **regular**, pero **cuesta** más dinero comprar las cosas. **Para mí**, es muy divertido comprar todas las cosas que me **gustan**. Por ejemplo, compro ropa, zapatos, **joyas**, **relojes**, **gafas para sol** y **perfumes**. Encuentro de todo esto en el centro comercial.

Es divertido comprar todo este tipo de cosas. **Sin embargo**, todo eso cuesta dinero. Entonces, **necesito** dinero para comprar todas estas cosas que me gustan. Primeramente, puedo **utilizar** mi **tarjeta de crédito**. Con mi tarjeta de crédito, puedo pagar las cosas que quiero comprar. Pero, debo pagar el **balance** de la tarjeta al **final del mes**. **De lo contrario**, tengo que pagar **intereses**. Además, puedo tener **problemas** por el **retraso** en el pago de la tarjeta.

La otra forma de pagar mis compras es con **dinero en efectivo**. Esta es la forma más **segura** puesto que **uso** mi dinero y listo. No tengo **deuda** en mi tarjeta de crédito. Pagar con dinero en efectivo es mejor que pagar con un **cheque**. No todas las tiendas aceptan cheques. Entonces, es mucho más seguro usar efectivo, o bien, mi tarjeta de crédito.

Para tener dinero, necesito **ganarlo**. Hay muchas formas de ganarse el dinero. Se puede tener un **empleo** en donde se recibe un **salario**, un **negocio** en donde se **obtienen ingresos**, o se puede ganar el dinero en la **lotería**. Todos soñamos con ganar la lotería, aunque esto no es algo **realista**. Son muy **afortunados** los que tienen la suerte de ganarse la lotería.

En mi caso, yo trabajo. Tengo un empleo en una **oficina**. En este empleo, trabajo de **lunes** a **viernes**. Tengo un salario **mensual** que recibo **quincenalmente**. Mi **sueldo** no es muy alto, pero tampoco es muy bajo. Me **alcanza** para todos mis gastos. Luego, **ahorro** un poco de dinero, y el resto lo puedo usar para comprar las cosas que tanto me gustan.

Este mes, hay muchas ofertas. Se viene el cambio de **temporada**. Cuando hay cambio de temporada, las tiendas bajan sus precios para todas **aquellas mercancías** que están **fuera de moda**. Es una buena oportunidad para **conseguir** cosas muy bonitas a un precio **fantástico**. Además, el dinero que tengo me alcanza para comprar más cosas.

Estoy pensando en comprarme un nuevo **sombrero** para la **playa**. Me gusta mucho ir a la playa, pero quiero un sombrero nuevo. Seguramente **encontraré** uno que me guste. Ya tengo mis gafas de sol y el atuendo que **usaré**. Solo me hace falta un lindo sombrero.

Mis amigas también están emocionadas con las ofertas. Ellas tienen gustos **similares** a los **míos**. Entonces, creo que nos divertiremos mucho en el centro comercial. Creo que será un fin de semana increíble. Lo único malo del fin de semana es que se **termina**... el lunes debo **volver** a mi trabajo. Pero no importa. Soy muy **feliz** porque tengo un buen empleo.

Me siento muy **afortunada** de tener un buen empleo ya que hay muchas personas **desempleadas**. Una persona desempleada es aquella que no tiene un empleo. Entonces, está en **búsqueda** de una oportunidad **laboral**. Estas personas tienen muchos problemas **económicos**. Es por ello que me siento muy afortunada de **contar** con un buen empleo **todos los días**.

Resumen de la historia

Me gusta ir de compras los fines de semana en el centro comercial. Compro ropa, zapatos, joyas, gafas de sol, relojes y perfumes. Es muy divertido ir al centro comercial cuando hay ofertas de todo tipo, especialmente en el cambio de temporada.

Para pagar las cosas que me gustan, puedo utilizar mi tarjeta de crédito. También puedo pagar mis compras con dinero en efectivo. El dinero en efectivo es más seguro que pagar con cheque. Además, debo pagar mi tarjeta de crédito cada mes. De lo contrario, puedo tener muchos problemas por no pagar a tiempo.

Tengo un empleo con el cual gano un sueldo. Este sueldo me sirve para cubrir mis gastos y comprar las cosas que me gustan. También ahorro una parte de mi sueldo. Así, puedo ir de compras los fines de semana tranquilamente.

Este fin de semana hay muchas ofertas en el centro comercial por el cambio de temporada. En esta época, las tiendas bajan el precio a los productos que ya no están de moda. En este caso, es posible obtener bonitas mercancías a buen precio. Entonces, mi dinero me alcanza para comprar más cosas de las que me gustan.

Summary of the Story

I like shopping on weekends at the mall. I buy clothes, shoes, jewelry, sunglasses, watches, and perfumes. It is very fun to go to the mall when there are offers of all kinds, especially at the end of the season.

To pay for the things I like, I can use my credit card. I can also pay for my purchases with cash. Cash is safer than paying by check. In addition, I must pay my credit card every month. Otherwise, I may have many problems for not paying on time.

I have a job with which I earn a salary. This salary helps me cover my expenses and buy the things I like. I also save a part of my salary. So, I can go shopping on weekends confidently.

This weekend, there are many offers in the mall due to the end of the season. At this time, stores lower the price for products that are no longer in fashion. In this case, it is possible to obtain beautiful goods at a good price. Then, my money is enough to buy more of the things that I like.

Vocabulary

1. **favoritas**	favorites
2. **salir de compras**	shopping
3. **preferido**	favorite
4. **centro comercial**	Mall
5. **enorme**	huge
6. **cerca**	near
7. **Ahí**	There
8. **tiendas**	stores
9. **ropa**	clothing
10. **zapatos**	shoes
11. **disfrutamos**	We enjoy
12. **especialmente**	especially
13. **ofertas**	offers
14. **artículos**	articles
15. **precio**	price
16. **bonitas**	pretty
17. **regular**	regular
18. **cuesta**	cost
19. **Para m**	For m
20. **gustan**	like
21. **joyas**	jewelry
22. **relojes**	clocks
23. **gafas para sol**	Sunglasses
24. **perfumes**	perfumes
25. **Sin embargo**	But nevertheless
26. **necesito**	I need
27. **utilizar**	use

28. **tarjeta de crédito** credit card
29. **balance** balance
30. **final del mes** end of the month
31. **De lo contrario** On the contrary
32. **intereses** interests
33. **problemas** problems
34. **retraso** delay
35. **dinero en efectivo** cash
36. **segura** safe
37. **uso** use
38. **deuda** debt
39. **cheque** check
40. **ganarlo** earn it
41. **empleo** job
42. **salario** salary
43. **negocio** deal
44. **obtienen** they get
45. **ingresos** income
46. **lotería** lottery
47. **realista** realistic
48. **afortunados** lucky ones
49. **En mi caso** In my case
50. **oficina** office
51. **lunes** Monday
52. **viernes** Friday
53. **mensual** monthly
54. **quincenalmente** fortnightly
55. **sueldo** salary
56. **alcanza** achieves

57. **ahorro** saving

58. **temporada** season

59. **aquellas** those

60. **mercancías** goods

61. **fuera de moda** out of style

62. **conseguir** get

63. **fantástico** fantastic

64. **sombrero** hat

65. **playa** Beach

66. **encontraré** I'll find

67. **usaré** will wear

68. **similares** Similar

69. **míos** mine

70. **termina** ends

71. **volver** return

72. **feliz** happy

73. **Me siento** I feel

74. **afortunada** lucky

75. **desempleadas** unemployed

76. **búsqueda** search

77. **laboral** labor

78. **económicos** cheap

79. **contar** tell

80. **todos los días** everyday

Questions About the Story

1. ¿Qué compro cuando voy de compras?
    a. Comida
    b. Ropa
    c. Autos
    d. Cheques
2. ¿Cómo pagos las cosas que compro?
    a. Con una tarjeta decrédito
    b. Con una tarjeta decheque
    c. Con una tarjeta de negocios
    d. Con una tarjeta de presentación
3. ¿Cuándo debo pagar mi tarjeta decrédito?
    a. Al final de la semana
    b. Al final del día
    c. Al final del domingo
    d. Al final del mes
4. ¿Cómo gano dinero?
    a. En la lotería
    b. Con suerte
    c. Dentro de mi casa
    d. Con mi empleo
5. ¿Cuándo hay ofertas en el centro comercial?
    a. Hoy y mañana

b. La próxima semana

c. Pronto hay ofertas

d. Este fin de semana

Answers

1. B
2. A
3. D
4. D
5. D

Chapter Nine

Everyone's Job Is Important — El trabajo de todos es importante

En nuestra **comunidad**, el **trabajo** de todos es importante. Todas las personas **hacen** un trabajo **significativo**. **Sin** su trabajo, nuestra comunidad no **podría funcionar adecuadamente**. Esto hace de cada trabajo, un trabajo esencial para el **bienestar** de la comunidad.

Hay **algunos** trabajos que son **vitales** para nuestra comunidad. Por ejemplo, la **policía**, **bomberos** y **paramédicos** son trabajos **imprescindibles**. Sin estos trabajos, nuestra comunidad no tendría personas para responder en caso de una **emergencia**. Es por ello que estas personas son **verdaderos héroes** en **nuestra** comunidad.

Otros empleos importantes son los **maestros**. Ellos **preparan** a los **niños** hoy, para ser **líderes mañana**. Los niños son **valiosos** para la comunidad y nuestro país. Por eso, **debemos cuidar** de ellos. Debemos cuidar también de los maestros que les **enseñan** cosas **útiles** y **positivas**.

Luego, **existe** otro tipo de **empleos** que son **igualmente** de importantes. Estos empleos se **encargan** de **asegurar** del buen **funcionamiento** de nuestra ciudad. Estos son **trabajadores públicos**. Ellos se aseguran de limpiar la ciudad. También se **aseguran** de **mantener** los servicios básicos funcionando tales como el **agua**, la **electricidad** y la **recolección** de **basura**. Su trabajo es tan importante como **cualquier** otro.

Otro tipo de empleos en nuestra ciudad son los trabajos **profesionales**. Estos empleos incluyen a los **ingenieros**, **abogados**, **arquitectos**, **contadores** y **gerentes**. Todos ellos ofrecen sus **conocimientos** para el desarrollo de nuestra comunidad y nuestro **país**. Ellos deben estudiar muchos años en la **universidad** para alcanzar el conocimiento que necesitan en su empleo.

Un trabajo profesional de **alta importancia** es ser **doctor**. Los doctores, o médicos, son personas que atienden a aquellos que están **enfermos** o **heridos**. **Regularmente**, trabajan en un **hospital** o en una **clínica**. Los médicos, junto con las **enfermeras**, son personas muy **nobles** que siempre están al servicio de las personas que los necesitan. Es por ello que los médicos y las enfermeras trabajan juntos para **brindar** la atención que una persona necesita en caso de una emergencia.

Otro de los trabajos que son altamente importantes para nuestra comunidad son los **agricultores**. Los agricultores, o **granjeros**, son aquellos que se encargan de producir los alimentos que **comemos** diariamente. Sin su trabajo, no

tendríamos alimentos. Por lo tanto, su trabajo es tan importante como el de cualquier otra persona. Los granjeros producen **frutas** y **vegetales** al igual que **crían** los animales que consumimos. Entonces, el trabajo del agricultor es **fundamental** para el bienestar de nuestra comunidad.

Y tú, ¿**cuál** es tu trabajo?

Seguramente tu trabajo es tan importante como el de **cualquier** otra persona. Sin tu trabajo, tu comunidad no puede vivir bien. No importa cual es tu trabajo. Lo que importa es que tu trabajo es tan importante como cualquier otro. **Por lo tanto**, debes hacerlo lo mejor posible. Si haces tu trabajo con una actitud positiva, los resultados también serán positivos. Tendrás **buenos resultados** en tu empleo. Tu comunidad estará **agradecida** con tu **esfuerzo**.

En cuanto a mi empleo, yo soy un **mecánico**. Yo trabajo **arreglando** los autos de los **demás**. Cuando alguien tiene un problema con su auto, me **pide** ayuda. Yo **reviso** el auto y lo **reparo**. Muchas veces, los autos **solamente** necesitan servicio. Algunas veces, es necesario **cambiar** una **pieza** que está mala. Mi trabajo requiere de conocimiento sobre el funcionamiento de los autos. Pero con **experiencia**, **sé** mucho. Las personas me agradecen mi trabajo porque sus autos están **funcionando** bien.

Me gusta mucho mi trabajo. Lo hago **felizmente**. Me gusta ver cuando una persona está feliz de que su auto está en buenas condiciones. Muchas veces, no fácil repararlo. Pero con un poco de esfuerzo, **pronto** está funcionando al **cien por ciento**.

Resumen de la historia

En nuestra comunidad, todos los trabajos son importantes. Todos tienen un trabajo valioso. Pero, hay algunos trabajos que son esenciales para el funcionamiento de nuestra comunidad. Por ejemplo, la policía, los bomberos y los paramédicos son muy importantes para la seguridad de las personas.

También hay otros trabajos sumamente útiles. Los maestros son los encargados de enseñar a los niños. Los niños son los futuros líderes de nuestra comunidad. Los doctores y enfermeras son vitales ya que atienden a las personas que están enfermas o heridas. Su trabajo salva las vidas de las personas.

Luego, existen trabajos llamados "profesionales". Estas personas ayudan al desarrollo de nuestra comunidad y país. Algunos son ingenieros, arquitectos abogados o contadores. Ellos están a cargo de puestos importantes dentro de nuestra comunidad.

Hacer un trabajo con una actitud positiva es fundamental para ayudar a las personas. Cuando se hace un trabajo de la mejor manera posible, se lograr alcanzar el éxito. Además, se ayuda a las personas en la comunidad. Nuestra comunidad y país son mejores gracias a nuestro trabajo bien hecho. Tu comunidad y tu familia aprecian el trabajo que haces cada día. Tu trabajo es esencial para tu comunidad.

Summary of the Story

In our community, all jobs are important. Everyone has a valuable job. But, there are some jobs that are essential for the functioning of our community. For example, police, firefighters, and paramedics are very important for the safety of people.

There are also other extremely useful jobs. Teachers are in charge of teaching children. Children are the future leaders of our community. Doctors and nurses are important, as they care for people who are sick or injured. Their work saves people's lives.

Then, there are jobs called "professional." These people help with the development of our community and country. Some are engineers, architects, lawyers, or accountants. They are in charge of important positions within our community.

Doing a job with a positive attitude is essential to help people. When a job is done in the best possible way, success is achieved. In addition, it helps people in the community. Our community and country are better, thanks to our work done well. Your community and your family appreciate the work you do every day. Your work is essential to your community.

Vocabulary

1. **comunidad**	community
2. **trabajo**	work
3. **hacen**	make
4. **significativo**	significant
5. **sin**	without
6. **podría**	might
7. **funcionar**	function
8. **adecuadamente**	adequately
9. **bienestar**	wellness
10. **algunos**	some
11. **vitales**	vital
12. **policía**	police
13. **bomberos**	firefighters
14. **paramédicos**	paramedics
15. **imprescindibles**	essential
16. **emergencia**	emergency
17. **verdaderos**	true
18. **héroes**	heroes
19. **nuestra**	our
20. **otros**	others
21. **maestros**	teachers
22. **preparan**	prepare
23. **niños**	children
24. **líderes**	leaders
25. **mañana**	morning
26. **valiosos**	valuable
27. **debemos**	we must

28. **cuidar**	look after
29. **enseñan**	they teach
30. **útiles**	tools
31. **positivas**	positive
32. **existe**	exists
33. **empleos**	jobs
34. **igualmente**	equally
35. **encargan**	commission
36. **asegurar**	ensure
37. **funcionamiento**	functioning
38. **trabajadores públicos**	public workers
39. **aseguran**	ensure
40. **mantener**	keep
41. **agua**	water
42. **electricidad**	electricity
43. **recolección**	harvest
44. **basura**	trash
45. **cualquier**	any
46. **profesionales**	professionals
47. **ingenieros**	engineers
48. **abogados**	lawyers
49. **arquitectos**	architects
50. **contadores**	counters
51. **gerentes**	managers
52. **conocimientos**	knowledge
53. **país**	country
54. **universidad**	college
55. **alta importancia**	high importance
56. **doctor**	doctor

57. **enfermos** sick
58. **heridos** wounded
59. **regularmente** regularly
60. **hospital** hospital
61. **clínica** clinic
62. **enfermeras** nurses
63. **nobles** noble
64. **brindar** offer
65. **agricultores** farmers
66. **granjeros** farmers
67. **comemos** we eat
68. **tendríamos** we would have
69. **frutas** fruits
70. **vegetales** vegetables
71. **crían** breed
72. **fundamental** fundamental
73. **cuál** which
74. **cualquier** any
75. **por lo tanto** thus
76. **buenos** good ones
77. **resultados** results
78. **agradecida** grateful
79. **esfuerzo** effort
80. **mecánico** mechanic
81. **arreglando** fixing up
82. **demás** the rest
83. **pide** asks
84. **reviso** revised
85. **reparo** repair

86. **solamente**	only
87. **cambiar**	change
88.**pieza**	piece
89. **experiencia**	experience
90.**sé**	he
91. **funcionando**	running
92. **felizmente**	happily
93. **pronto**	soon
94. **cien por ciento**	hundred percent

Questions About the Story

1. ¿Cuáles son los trabajos importantes en la comunidad?
    a. Algunos trabajos
    b. Unos pocos trabajos
    c. Todos los trabajos
    d. Casi todos los trabajos
2. ¿Cuáles trabajos son esenciales para la comunidad?
    a. Policía, bomberos y mecánicos.
    b. Policía, bomberos y profesionales
    c. Policía, bomberos y paramédicos
    d. Policía, bomberos y arquitectos
3. ¿Quiénes enseñan a los niños?
    a. Los maestros
    b. Los doctores
    c. Los ingenieros
    d. Los abogados
4. ¿Qué se necesita para hacer un buen trabajo?
    a. Buenas intenciones
    b. Algunas ideas
    c. Actitud positiva
    d. Actividad física
5. ¿Para quién es esencial tu trabajo?
    a. Para tu comunidad

b. Para el gobierno

c. Para la empresa

d. Para los nuevos

Answers

1. C
2. C
3. A
4. C
5. A

Chapter Ten

The World of Sport — El mundo de los deportes

Los **deportes** son una de las **pasiones** más grandes de las personas en todo el mundo. Cuando una persona es **aficionada** a un deporte, también se le **conoce** como "fan" de ese deporte. **En la actualidad**, **existen** una gran **cantidad** de deportes. Cada deporte tiene sus propias **características** que los hacen **atractivos** para los fans.

Primeramente, los deportes se **dividen** en **individuales** y en **equipo**. Un deporte individual es aquel en donde una persona **sola** practica el deporte sin la ayuda de otra persona. Por ejemplo, el **golf**, **tenis**, **natación** y **ciclismo** con algunos de los deportes individuales. En el caso del tenis, es posible jugar en **parejas**. **Sin embargo**, **solamente** es necesario una persona para **realizar** el deporte.

Los deportes individuales son ideales para **aquellas** personas que no tienen mucho **tiempo** para **formar** parte de un equipo. **En este caso**, la persona puede practicar el deporte en su tiempo libre. **En muchos casos**, no se necesitan **implementos deportivos**. **Simplemente** se necesita la **voluntad** de la persona que desea practicar el deporte.

Uno de los deportes más fáciles de practicar es el **atletismo**. En particular, **correr** es un deporte fácil y **sencillo** de realizar. **Básicamente**, el atleta únicamente necesita un **par** de **zapatillas deportivas** para realizarlo. Claro, se requiere de **esfuerzo** y **dedicación**. Aun así, la persona únicamente debe ponerse sus zapatillas y listo.

Luego, los deportes en equipo son aquellos en donde se necesita una cantidad **específica** de **jugadores** para realizar el deporte **apropiadamente**. Algunos ejemplos de este tipo de deportes son el **fútbol**, **basquetbol**, **volibol**, **béisbol**, y **rugby**. La cantidad de jugadores por equipo **varía** según el deporte. Además, en todos estos deportes se tienen dos equipos que se enfrentan en una **partida**. El resultado se determina **de acuerdo** con la cantidad de **puntos** que **acumula** cada equipo.

Usualmente, los deportes en equipo **requieren** de implementos y algún tipo de **cancha**. En el caso de fútbol, **únicamente** se necesita un **balón**. En el caso de otros deportes, se requiere de muchos implementos deportivos. **En algunos casos**, se requiere de una cancha especializada para la práctica de este deporte. En el caso del basquetbol, se requiere de una cancha con las **cestas** para realizar este juego.

En todos los deportes que existen, hay **ciertas reglas** que los **participantes** deben seguir. Las reglas son la forma **correcta** de practicar este deporte. Si no se **siguen** las reglas adecuadamente, no se practica el deporte **correctamente**. Es por ello que todos los participantes deben conocer las reglas **claramente**. Algunos deportes tienen reglas sencillas, como es el caso del rugby, mientras que existen otros deportes con reglas **complejas** como es el caso del **fútbol americano**.

En prácticamente todos los deportes existe un **árbitro**. Un árbitro es una persona **imparcial** que **controla** el juego, **es decir**, es la persona encargada de asegurarse de las reglas del juego. Si algún participante **rompe** las reglas, el árbitro se encarga de **corregir** la situación. El trabajo del árbitro es muy difícil especialmente cuando los jugadores del juego no están **de acuerdo** con las **decisiones** que el árbitro toma.

Todos los deportes tienen sus propias características que los hace **únicos**. Cada persona escoge ser fan del deporte que más le gusta. **Aun así**, hay personas que **prefieren** no ver o participar en algún deporte. Eso está bien. Lo importante es poder **apreciar** la **belleza** de cada deporte y **apoyar** a los atletas que los practican. Cuando se practica un deporte con pasión, realmente se disfruta formar parte de una experiencia singular en la vida.

Y tú, ¿cuál es tu deporte favorito? ¿Practicas algún deporte? Por salud y bienestar físico siempre es bueno practicar algún deporte; no importa cual.

Resumen de la historia

Existen muchas diferentes clases de deportes. En particular, existen dos tipos de deportes, individuales y en equipo. Cada deporte tiene sus aficionados. Cuando una persona es aficionada a un deporte se le llama “fan”.

Los deportes individuales son aquellos en donde una sola persona puede practicar el deporte. Es decir, no se necesitan de más personas para llevar a cabo la práctica del deporte. Estos deportes incluyen la natación, el ciclismo, el golf y el tenis. En algunos casos, se pueden practicar los deportes en parejas como es el caso del tenis.

Además, los deportes individuales no requieren de muchos implementos deportivos. Muchas veces, se necesita muy poco para practicarlos. Por ejemplo, correr básicamente requiere de un par de zapatillas deportivas nada más.

En el caso de los deportes en equipo, se necesita de una cantidad específica de personas, o jugadores, para realizar el deporte apropiadamente. Algunos de estos deportes son el fútbol, rugby, béisbol y basquetbol. En algunos casos, se necesita de una cancha especializada para realizar estos deportes. En el basquetbol, se necesita una cancha con dos cestas para realizar el deporte correctamente.

El árbitro es la persona encargada del cumplimiento de las reglas del juego. Cuando un jugador rompe las reglas, el árbitro debe asegurar que el juego continúe correctamente.

Summary of the Story

There are many different kinds of sports. In particular, there are two types of sports, individual and team sports. Every sport has its fans. When a person is fond of a sport, they are called a "fan."

Individual sports are those where only one person can practice the sport. That is, no more people are needed to carry out the practice of the sport. These sports include swimming, cycling, golf, and tennis. In some cases, sports can be practiced in pairs such as in tennis.

In addition, individual sports do not require many sports equipment. Many times, very little is needed to practice them. For example, running basically requires a pair of sneakers and nothing more.

In the case of team sports, a specific number of people or players are needed to perform the sport properly. Some of these sports are football, rugby, baseball, and basketball. In some cases, a specialized court is needed to perform these sports. In basketball, a court with two baskets is needed to perform the sport correctly.

The referee is the person in charge of compliance with the rules of the game. When a player breaks the rules, the referee must ensure that the game continues correctly.

Vocabulary

1. **deportes**	sports
2. **pasiones**	passions
3. **aficionada**	amateur
4. **conoce**	known
5. **En la actualidad**	nowadays
6. **existen**	exist
7. **cantidad**	quantity
8. **características**	characteristics
9. **atractivos**	attractive
10. **dividen**	divide
11. **individuales**	individual
12. **equipo**	team
13. **sola**	alone
14. **golf**	golf
15. **tenis**	tennis
16. **natación**	swimming
17. **ciclismo**	cycling
18. **parejas**	couples
19. **Sin embargo**	but nevertheless
20. **solamente**	only
21. **realizar**	perform
22. **aquellas**	those
23. **tiempo**	weather
24. **formar**	to form
25. **En este caso**	in this case
26. **En muchos casos**	in many cases
27. **implementos deportivos**	sports equipment

28. **Simplemente**	simply
29. **voluntad**	will
30. **atletismo**	athletics
31. **correr**	run
32. **sencillo**	simple
33. **Básicamente**	basically
34. **par**	pair
35. **zapatillas deportivas**	sneakers
36. **esfuerzo**	effort
37. **dedicación**	dedication
38. **específica**	specific
39. **jugadores**	players
40. **apropiadamente**	properly
41. **fútbol**	football
42. **basquetbol**	basketball
43. **volibol**	volleyball
44. **béisbol**	baseball
45. **rugby**	rugby
46. **varía**	it varies
47. **partida**	departure
48. **de acuerdo**	in agreement
49. **puntos**	points
50. **acumula**	accumulates
51. **Usualmente**	usually
52. **requieren**	require
53. **cancha**	court
54. **únicamente**	only
55. **balón**	ball
56. **En algunos casos**	In some cases

57. **cestas**	baskets
58. **ciertas**	true
59. **reglas**	rules
60.**participantes**	participants
61. **correcta**	correct
62. **siguen**	follow
63. **correctamente**	correctly
64. **claramente**	clearly
65. **complejas**	complex
66. **fútbol americano**	football
67. **árbitro**	referee
68. **imparcial**	impartial
69. **controla**	controls
70. **es decir**	that is to say
71. **rompe**	breaker
72. **corregir**	to correct
73. **de acuerdo**	in agreement
74. **decisiones**	decisions
75. **únicos**	unique
76. **Aun así**	Even so
77. **prefieren**	prefer
78. **apreciar**	to appreciate
79. **belleza**	beauty
80.**apoyar**	support

Questions About the Story

1. ¿A quién se le llama "fan"?
    a. A un árbitro
    b. A un aficionado
    c. A un jugador
    d. A un profesional
2. ¿Cuáles son los deportes individuales?
    a. Aquellos que se practican individualmente
    b. Aquellos que se hacen en grupo
    c. Aquellos que no usan implementos deportivos
    d. Aquellos que se practican de día
3. ¿Cuáles son los deportes en equipo?
    a. Aquellos que se practican individualmente
    b. Aquellos que se hacen en grupo
    c. Aquellos que no usan implementos deportivos
    d. Aquellos que se practican de día
4. ¿Qué son los implementos deportivos?
    a. El equipo necesario para practicar el deporte
    b. Las personas necesarias para el juego
    c. El árbitro imparcial en la cancha de juego
    d. Los aficionados que apoyan al equipo
5. ¿Quién es el árbitro?
    a. Es la persona que controla el juego

b. Es uno de los jugadores del equipo

c. Es quien tiene el balón de juego

d. Es el individuo que practica deporte

Answers

1. B
2. A
3. B
4. A
5. A

Chapter Eleven

Hobbies — Los pasatiempos

El tiempo libre es el tiempo en que no se trabaja ni se va a la escuela. **Durante** este tiempo, las personas **acostumbran** a realizar **varias** actividades. Algunas de las actividades más comunes son salir con amigos, ver televisión, **leer** un libro o **simplemente** descansar en casa. Es importante **aprovechar** el tiempo libre especialmente cuando se trabaja muy **duro**. Para muchas personas, el tiempo libre es muy **valioso**.

Una de las actividades que se pueden realizar en el tiempo libre es un **pasatiempo**. Un pasatiempo es una actividad que se realiza **específicamente** en el tiempo libre. Si realizas alguna de estas actividades como parte de tu trabajo **habitual**, entonces no es un pasatiempo.

Un pasatiempo es una actividad **divertida** en la cual una persona realiza una **acción** que disfruta **muchísimo**. Existen muchísimas actividades que se **consideran** como pasatiempo. Éstas son algunas de las actividades que se realizan como parte de los pasatiempos: **coleccionar artículos**, **tejer**, **escribir**, **pintar**, **construir modelos**, **la jardinería**, **cocinar**, practicar un deporte, **tocar un instrumento musical**, o bien viajar. Cualquier de estas actividades, entre tantas más, se consideran como pasatiempos.

Otra palabra para **referirse** a un pasatiempo es "hobby". Cuando realizas un pasatiempo, tu **cuerpo** y **mente** se **transportan** a un lugar en donde estás totalmente **concentrado** en la actividad que realizas. Esto es lo que hace de los pasatiempos, una actividad **placentera**. Por eso, si tienes algún hobby, lo puedes hacer con toda la motivación posible.

A muchas personas les gusta coleccionar algún artículo. El tipo de artículos coleccionables varía grandemente. Por ejemplo, hay personas que coleccionan **vasos**, **platos**, **monedas** o bien **estampillas postales**. Otras personas coleccionan **antigüedades**, es decir, artículos muy **viejos** que tienen un alto **valor** histórico. Las antigüedades, por lo general, son **costosas** ya que cuentan con muchos años de historia.

Los coleccionistas pasan mucho tiempo viajando de **sitio** en sitio en **búsqueda** de los artículos que coleccionan. En algunos casos, conocen a otras personas que se **dedican** a buscar los artículos coleccionables para luego **revenderlos** a los coleccionistas.

Otras personas realizan pasatiempos como **cocinar**. Cocinar es una **tarea** muy común ya que todos **debemos** comer. **Sin embargo**, hay personas que les gusta cocinar como una **manera** de **expresar** sus **habilidades artísticas**. Entonces, se dedican a preparar **platillos** nuevos en donde sus amigos y familias pueden **saborear** nuevas **creaciones**. Algunas otras personas disfrutan preparar platillos de diferentes países del mundo. Con esto, pueden **experimentar** con nuevos sabores.

Algunas personas practican algún deporte a manera de pasatiempo. Cuando se practica un deporte, no se **tiene** en mente **competir**. Por el contrario, se practica el deporte por el **amor** el juego. Como tal, estas personas buscan compartir con amigos y **pasarla** bien **durante** el juego.

Un pasatiempo **increíble** es viajar. Existen personas que tiene tiempo y dinero por lo que buscan nuevos lugares por **conocer**. Estas personas van de ciudad en ciudad, o de país en país, en búsqueda de nuevas **aventuras**. Estas aventuras pueden ser conocer sitios históricos, **monumentos antiguos**, o descubrir leyendas de otras culturas. En definitiva, viajar es uno de los pasatiempos más **emocionantes**.

Personalmente, mi pasatiempo es coleccionar **fotografías**. Me gusta mucho tomar fotografías. Tengo una **camera** con la que voy por todas partes. Tomo fotos de todas las cosas que encuentro. Me gusta tomar fotos a las personas, a las mascotas y a los paisajes. En particular, me gusta tomar foto del **amanecer**. El **cielo** se pone **hermoso** cuando el sol sale en la **mañana**.

Tengo miles de fotos. Tomo muchísimas fotos **cada vez** que viajo. Estos son **recuerdos** para siempre. **No quiero olvidar** ni un **momento** de mis viajes. Son **experiencias** que nunca **olvidaré**. Tengo muchos recuerdos de distintos lugares. Pero, mi lugar favorito es un **volcán activo**. Estar cerca de un volcán activo es una experiencia alucinante. Es ideal para los amantes de la aventura.

No sé a dónde haré mi **siguiente** viaje. Lo que sí estoy seguro es que tomaré muchas fotos. Este es mi pasatiempo. Tomar fotografías de todas las cosas y personas **maravillosas** que encuentro por todas partes. Lo mejor de todo es que es un pasatiempo que puedo compartir con mis amigos y mi familia. A todos les **encantan** mis fotos.

Resumen de la historia

Los pasatiempos son actividades que se realizan cuando no se trabaja. Es por ello que un pasatiempo es una actividad divertida que es agradable para la persona que la practica. Si se realizan estas actividades como parte del trabajo de una persona, entonces no es un pasatiempo.

Algunos ejemplos de pasatiempos son coleccionar artículos, cocinar, tejer, o construir modelos de algún tipo. Algunas otras personas disfrutan practicar deportes a manera de pasatiempo. Estas personas hacen deporte por amor al juego y no por deseo de competir en dicho deporte.

Los pasatiempos artísticos son una oportunidad para mostrar las habilidades de una persona. Estos pasatiempos incluyen la pintura, escritura y la música. Uno de los pasatiempos más impresionantes es viajar. Conocer nuevos lugares es una experiencia singular en la vida. Las personas que viajan mucho son muy afortunadas porque conocer muchos lugares nuevos y muchas personas especiales.

Personalmente, mi pasatiempo es la fotografía. Me encanta tomar fotografías de todos los lugares a donde voy. Estos son recuerdos que me quedan de cada una de mis aventuras. Tengo miles de fotos que comparto con mis amigos y mi familia. A

ellos les encantan mis fotos. También me encanta tomar fotografías de cada uno de los lugares nuevos que visito.

Summary of the Story

Hobbies are activities that are done when you don't work. That is why a hobby is a fun activity that is enjoyable for the person who practices it. If these activities are performed as part ofa person's work, then they are not a hobby.

Some examples of hobbies are collecting items, cooking, knitting, or building models of some kind. Other people enjoy playing sports as a hobby. These people play sports for the love of the game and not for the desire to compete in that sport.

Artistic hobbies are an opportunity to show a person's skills. These hobbies include painting, writing, and music. One of the most impressive hobbies is traveling. Knowing new places is a unique experience in life. People who travel a lot are very lucky because they know many new places and many special people.

Personally, my hobby is photography. I love taking pictures of all the places I go. These are memories that I have left of each of my adventures. I have thousands of photos that I share with my friends and family. They love my photos. I also love taking pictures of each of the new places I visit.

Vocabulary

1. **durante**	during
2. **acostumbran**	get used
3. **varias**	several
4. **leer**	read
5. **simplemente**	simply
6. **aprovechar**	to take advantage of
7. **duro**	hard
8. **valioso**	valuable
9. **pasatiempo**	hobby
10. **específicamente**	specifically
11. **habitual**	habitual
12. **divertida**	funny
13. **acción**	action
14. **muchísimo**	very much
15. **consideran**	consider
16. **coleccionar artículos**	collect items
17. **tejer**	to knit
18. **escribir**	to write
19. **pintar**	paint
20. **construir modelos**	build models
21. **la jardinería**	the garden
22. **cocinar**	cook
23. **tocar un instrumento musical**	play a musical instrument
24. **referirse**	refer
25. **cuerpo**	body
26. **mente**	mind

27. **transportan**	transport
28. **concentrado**	concentrated
29. **placentera**	pleasant
30. **vasos**	glasses
31. **platos**	dishes
32. **monedas**	coins
33. **estampillas postales**	postal stamps
34. **antigüedades**	antiques
35. **viejos**	old
36. **valor**	value
37. **costosas**	expensive
38. **sitio**	site
39. **búsqueda**	search
40. **dedican**	they dedicate
41. **revenderlos**	resell them
42. **cocinar**	cook
43. **tarea**	homework
44. **debemos**	we must
45. **sin embargo**	but nevertheless
46. **manera**	way
47. **expresar**	express
48. **habilidades**	skills
49. **artísticas**	artistic
50. **platillos**	dishes
51. **saborear**	savor
52. **creaciones**	creations
53. **experimentar**	to experience
54. **tiene**	has
55. **competir**	to compete

56. **amor**	love
57. **pasarla**	pass it
58. **durante**	during
59. **increíble**	incredible
60.**conocer**	know
61. **aventuras**	adventure
62. **monumentos**	monuments
63. **antiguos**	ancient
64. **emocionantes**	exciting
65. **personalmente**	personally
66. **fotografías**	photographs
67. **camera**	camera
68. **amanecer**	sunrise
69. **cielo**	sky
70. **hermoso**	beautiful
71. **mañana**	morning
72. **cada vez**	every time
73. **recuerdos**	memories
74. **no quiero**	I do not want
75. **olvidar**	forget
76. **momento**	moment
77. **experiencias**	experiences
78. **olvidaré**	I will forget
79. **volcán activo**	active volcano
80.**siguiente**	following
81. **maravillosas**	wonderful
82.**encantan**	love them

Questions About the Story

1. ¿Qué es un pasatiempo?
    a. Es una actividad importante
    b. Es una actividad en tiempo libre
    c. Es una actividad improductiva
    d. Es una actividad descriptiva
2. ¿Cómo son los pasatiempos?
    a. Son divertidos
    b. Son aburridos
    c. Son nuevos
    d. Son viejos
3. ¿Cuáles son algunos ejemplos de pasatiempos?
    a. Coleccionar viajes
    b. Coleccionar ropa
    c. Coleccionar estampillas
    d. Coleccionar mascotas
4. ¿Cuál es un pasatiempo impresionante?
    a. Viajar
    b. Comer
    c. Jugar
    d. Dormir
5. ¿Cuál es mi pasatiempo?
    a. La fotografía

b. La cocina

c. La comida

d. La labor

Answers

1. B
2. A
3. C
4. A
5. A

Chapter Twelve

The Importance of Banks — La importancia de los bancos

El dinero es muy importante en nuestras vidas. Nos **sirve** para **comprar** las cosas que **necesitamos** todos los días. Con el dinero podemos comprar comida, ropa, **medicina**, **gasolina** para el auto, pagar los **gastos de la casa** y **obtener** cualquier cosa que necesitamos.

En muchos casos, las personas obtienen dinero de su empleo. Cuando una persona tiene un empleo, **recibe** un **salario**. En algunos casos, existen personas que ganan un salario muy alto. Estas personas reciben más dinero cada mes. Otras personas, ganan un salario bajo, por ejemplo, ganan el **salario mínimo** en su país.

En otros casos, las personas que tienen un **negocio** ganan dinero de esta manera. Una persona que tiene un negocio se le conoce como "**emprendedor**". Un emprendedor es una persona que tiene una actividad en donde gana dinero por su **esfuerzo**. Esto puede ser un negocio, una **actividad artística**, o bien, es **inventor** de algún producto **útil** e **interesante**.

Cuando se recibe dinero, **usualmente** se recibe a través de un **banco**. Los bancos son **instituciones** en donde se **deposita** el dinero de una persona en una

cuenta. Una cuenta lleva el nombre de la **persona titular**. Esto quiere decir que el dinero que se encuentra depositado en esa cuenta es de la persona titular. Entonces, esta persona puede **depositar** más dinero en esta cuenta o **retirarlo** cuando lo necesita.

Lo **ventaja** más grande de tener el dinero en un banco es la **seguridad**. Muchas veces, tener dinero en un banco es más seguro que tener el dinero guardado en casa. Esto es importante **especialmente** si se trata de mucho dinero. Cuando una persona tiene mucho dinero, es mejor **guardarlo** en un banco. Así, no hay **preocupaciones** de que el dinero está en **riesgo**.

El **dinero en efectivo**, o **cash**, sirve para **comprar** y **vender**. Pero muchas veces, puede ser **peligroso** tener mucho dinero en efectivo. Es por ello que los bancos ofrecen una **tarjeta de débito**. Una tarjeta de débito es una tarjeta plástica que sirve para realizar **transacciones** en lugar de usar efectivo. Con esta tarjeta es posible evitar el uso de dinero en efectivo. Simplemente se utiliza para pagar y listo. Es igual a pagar con dinero en efectivo.

Otro tipo de tarjeta es la llamada "**tarjeta de crédito**". La diferencia entre una tarjeta de crédito y una tarjeta de débito es que la tarjeta de débito retira dinero **directamente** de la cuenta de una persona. La tarjeta de crédito no retira dinero de una cuenta, sino que es una clase de **préstamo** que tiene la persona

propietaria de la tarjeta. Esto quiere decir que puede pagar con esa tarjeta por cualquier compra que realiza.

Usualmente, los clientes que **poseen** una tarjeta de crédito reciben un **estado de cuenta** al final del mes. En ese caso, deben realizar el pago de las compras que realizan con su tarjeta de crédito. Para ello, se puede pagar con dinero en efectivo o con un **cheque** a favor del banco. Con esto, quedan pagada la cuenta del mes **anterior**.

Así mismo, un cheque es un **documento** que sirve para entregar dinero a una persona. Este documento es igual que el dinero en efectivo. La diferencia es que el documento no vale como dinero. El cheque sirve para recibir el dinero a cambio. Básicamente, un cheque es una **promesa** de que la persona que lo recibe tendrá el dinero a cambio.

Para cambiar un cheque, es necesario **acudir** a un banco. El banco recibe el cheque y revisa si hay **suficientes fondos** en la cuenta. Si la cuenta tiene suficiente dinero, entonces el dinero en efectivo es **entregado** a la persona que lo **porta**. Los cheques son muy útiles para evitar grandes cantidades de dinero efectivo ya que cargar mucho dinero en efectivo es peligroso.

Los bancos ofrecen un servicio a la comunidad. Claro, estos **servicios** no son **gratuitos** puesto que cobran por algunos de los servicios que prestan. Sin embargo, los bancos son necesarios para facilitar las transacciones que se realizan a diario. Sin los bancos, las personas tendrían que **cargar** mucho dinero en efectivo. Esto no sólo es peligroso, sino que es **incómodo**. Por eso, los bancos ofrecen una buena opción para el manejo responsable del dinero.

Resumen de la historia

El dinero es importante en nuestras vidas. Nos permite comprar y vender las cosas que necesitamos a diario. Con el dinero, podemos obtener todas aquellas cosas que usamos como ropa, comida, medicinas y la gasolina para el auto.

Los bancos son importantes porque ayuda a manejar el dinero de una manera más fácil. Por ejemplo, se utilizan las tarjetas de débito y crédito para la gestión del dinero. Una tarjeta de débito retira dinero de la cuenta de una persona. Una tarjeta de crédito es un tipo de préstamo. Entonces, la persona puede pagar con la tarjeta de crédito, pero luego debe pagar el balance al final del mes.

Cuando una persona recibe dinero, por ejemplo, su salario, recibe el dinero en un banco. Esto hace este proceso más cómodo y seguro. Tener mucho dinero en efectivo es peligroso. Entonces, recibir dinero en un banco es una forma más segura de realizar este tipo de transacciones.

Los cheques también son una parte importante de los servicios de un banco. Cuando una persona recibe un cheque, recibe una promesa de obtener el dinero en efectivo. Entonces, el portador del cheque debe ir al banco para cambiarlo y recibir el dinero a cambio. Un cheque es muy útil sobre todo cuando son cantidades muy grandes de dinero.

Summary of the Story

Money is important in our lives. It allows us to buy and sell the things we needon a daily basis. With money, we can get all those things we use, such as clothes, food, medicine, and gas for the car.

Banks are important because they help manage money in an easier way. For example, debit and credit cards are used for money management. A debit card withdraws money from a person's account. A credit card is a type of loan. The person can pay with the credit card, but then they must pay the balance at the end of the month.

When a person receives money, for example, their salary, they receive the money in a bank. This makes this process more comfortable and safer. Having a lot of cash is dangerous. So, receiving money in a bank is a safer way to carry out these types of transactions.

Checks are also an important part of a bank's services. When a person receives a check, they receive a promise to get the money in cash. Then, the bearer of the check must go to the bank to change it and receive the money in return. A check is very useful, especially when they are very large amounts of money.

Vocabulary

1. **sirve**	it serves
2. **comprar**	to buy
3. **necesitamos**	we need
4. **medicina**	medicine
5. **gasolina**	gasoline
6. **gastos de la casa**	household expenses
7. **obtener**	obtain
8. **recibe**	receives
9. **salario**	salary
10. **salario mínimo**	minimum salary
11. **negocio**	deal
12. **emprendedor**	entrepreneur
13. **esfuerzo**	effort
14. **actividad artística**	artistic activity
15. **inventor**	inventor
16. **útil**	Useful
17. **interesante**	interesting
18. **usualmente**	usually
19. **banco**	Bank
20. **instituciones**	institutions
21. **deposita**	deposit
22. **cuenta**	account
23. **persona titular**	titular person
24. **depositar**	to deposit
25. **retirarlo**	remove it
26. **ventaja**	advantage
27. **seguridad**	security

28. **especialmente**	especially
29. **guardarlo**	save it
30. **preocupaciones**	worries
31. **riesgo**	risk
32. **dinero en efectivo**	cash
33. **cash**	cash
34. **comprar**	to buy
35. **vender**	to sell
36. **peligroso**	dangerous
37. **tarjeta de débito**	debit
38. **transacciones**	transactions
39. **tarjeta de crédito**	credit card
40. **directamente**	directly
41. **préstamo**	loan
42. **propietaria**	owner
43. **poseen**	they own
44. **estado de cuenta**	account status
45. **cheque**	check
46. **anterior**	previous
47. **documento**	document
48. **promesa**	promise
49. **acudir**	go
50. **suficientes**	enough
51. **fondos**	money
52. **entregado**	delivered
53. **porta**	holder
54. **servicios**	services
55. **gratuitos**	free
56. **cargar**	load

57. **incómodo** uncomfortable

Questions About the Story

1. ¿Qué es importante en nuestras vidas?
    a. Los autos
    b. El dinero
    c. La lotería
    d. El teléfono
2. ¿Para qué sirve el dinero?
    a. Para conocer otros planetas
    b. Para vivir en la playa
    c. Para comprar lo que necesitamos
    d. Para determina el futuro
3. ¿Para qué sirve una tarjeta de débito?
    a. Para comer en un restaurante
    b. Para visitar un volcán activo
    c. Para obtener un auto nuevo
    d. Para retirar dinero de una cuenta
4. ¿Qué es una tarjeta de crédito?
    a. Es una tarjeta de plástico
    b. Es una tarjeta de negocios
    c. Es una tarjeta de presentación
    d. Es una tarjeta de dinero
5. ¿Qué es un cheque?
    a. Es un documento nuevo

b. Es una promesa de dinero

c. Es una manera anterior

d. Es la mejor forma para ti

Answers

1. B
2. C
3. D
4. A
5. B

Chapter Thirteen

How to Get a Job — Como obtener un empleo

Una **empresa** es una institución que se **dedica** a alguna actividad **productiva**. Estas actividades **difieren según** el tipo de empresa. Por ejemplo, una **fábrica** produce artículos mientras que una **tienda** vende artículos al público.

En cualquier tipo de empresa, se necesitan **empleados**. Los empleados son personas que trabajan para la empresa. Una persona que trabaja en una empresa obtiene un empleo. Para obtener un empleo, es **necesario** pasar por un **proceso**. Este proceso es **generalmente** el mismo.

Primeramente, una empresa hace pública una **oferta de trabajo**. Lugares comunes en donde se publican las ofertas de trabajo son el **periódico local**, en **internet** o en alguna **oficina de empleo**. Estas ofertas de empleo están **disponibles** para todas las personas que están en búsqueda de un empleo.

Cuando una persona interesada en obtener empleo ve una oferta, primero debe **revisar** si el empleo está de acuerdo con sus **capacidades**, **experiencia** y **entrenamiento**. Usualmente, una oferta de empleo indica toda la información: experiencia requerida, **habilidades** necesarias y conocimientos **esenciales**. Si la persona interesada en el puesto de trabajo cumple con estas especificaciones, puede **presentar** su **solicitud de empleo**.

Una **solicitud de empleo** es un documento en donde se **manifiesta formalmente** el interés de una persona por obtener un empleo. En la solicitud, una persona anota toda su información **relevante** y la **entrega** a la empresa. En una solicitud, un **candidato** adjunta su **curriculum vitae**. Este es un documento en donde indica su **experiencia**, **estudios** y cualquier otra información relevante para la empresa.

Las personas encargadas del **departamento** de **recursos humanos revisan** la solicitud y **determinan** si la persona **cumple** con los **requisitos** en la oferta. Si no cumple con los requisitos, su solitud es **rechazada**. Esto significa que no se toma en cuenta para el empleo.

Si el candidato sí cumple con los requisitos **indicados** en la oferta, entonces se procede a realizar una **entrevista de trabajo**. Una entrevista de trabajo consiste en una persona encargada de **reclutamiento**, es decir, de **contratar** a nuevos empleados y el candidato. Esta entrevista es una manera de conocer más de cerca a la persona que estará trabajando para la empresa.

Cuando se **lleva a cabo** una entrevista, el candidato debe presentarse de una manera adecuada. Usualmente, un candidato se presenta **bien vestido**, y con **copias** de los documentos que necesita para **acreditar** sus estudios y experiencia.

Así mismo, el reclutador tiene una **lista** de elementos que el candidato debe cumplir. Es muy común **rechazar** candidatos después de una entrevista. **Por lo general,** se entrevistan a varios candidatos hasta tener una lista de **finalistas**. En la **lista de finalistas**, regularmente tres, se realiza una segunda entrevista. Esta segunda entrevista es con **representantes** del departamento en donde trabajará el candidato.

Al terminar la segunda entrevista, el reclutador puede tomar una **decisión**. Esto puede resultar en un nuevo candidato contratado para el empleo. En algunos casos, se procede a realizar una tercera entrevista. Esto es común en empleos de **alto nivel** en donde el candidato tiene un alto grado de **responsabilidad**.

Al finalizar el proceso de reclutamiento, la empresa decide a quien contratar. El candidato ganador es **notificado** de su **selección**. Esto significa que tiene el empleo. La empresa, por su parte, **elabora** un **contrato**. El contrato contiene todas las condiciones en donde se especifica qué es lo que el empleado debe hacer, su **horario de trabajo**, sus **beneficios**, y lo más importante, su salario. Todos estos **términos** se pueden **negociar** durante la entrevista de trabajo. Si la empresa y el candidato están **de acuerdo**, se **firma** el contrato. Con la firma del contrato, el empleado es ahora un nuevo empleado de la empresa.

Si el empleo es para trabajar en el gobierno de un país, el proceso es muy similar. Usualmente, los requisitos para trabajar en el gobierno son más estrictos que en una **empresa privada**. Pero, el proceso de reclutamiento es prácticamente el mismo.

Una vez empieza a trabajar el nuevo empleado, debe esperar un **período** de tiempo antes de recibir su primer salario. Por lo regular, el nuevo empleado recibe su salario al final de su primer mes. Esto es importante tomarlo en **consideración**. Existen casos en donde los empleados reciben un pago **anticipado**. Pero usualmente deben esperar para recibir su primersueldo.

El proceso para obtener un nuevo empleo puede ser rápido, es decir, puede durar unos cuantos días. En algunas **situaciones**, este proceso puede **durar** semanas, sino hasta meses. Muchas veces, esto **depende** del tipo de trabajo que la persona realizará.

Resumen de la historia

El proceso para obtener un empleo consiste en varios pasos. Primero, una empresa publica una oferta de empleo. Esta oferta de empleo indica todas las condiciones del empleo. Así mismo, indica los requisitos que el candidato debe cumplir en términos de experiencia y estudios.

Cuando una persona está interesada en un empleo, puede presentar su solicitud de empleo. Esta solicitud es un documento en donde formalmente pide ser considerado para el empleo. El encargado de recursos humanos de una empresa revisa la solicitud, junto con el curriculum vitae del candidato, y decide si la acepta o la rechaza.

Si la solicitud es aceptada, el candidato pasa a una entrevista de empleo. Esta entrevista de empleo consiste en una reunión en donde el reclutador conocer más acerca del candidato. En una entrevista, se puede rechazar o aceptar a un candidato. Una entrevista también es una oportunidad para negociar los términos del empleo.

Cuando el candidato es contratado, debe firma un contrato. El contrato es el documento formal en donde se establecen todos los términos del empleado. Con la firma del contrato, el candidato ya tiene un nuevo empleo. Pero, deberá esperar un

tiempo para recibir su primer salario. Usualmente, debe esperar un mes antes de recibir su primer salario.

Summary of the Story

The process to obtain a job consists of several steps. First, a company publishes a job offer. This job offer indicates all conditions of employment. It also indicates the requirements that the candidate must meet in terms of experience and studies.

When a person is interested in a job, they can submit their job application. This application is a document where a candidate formally asks to be considered for employment. The human resources manager of a company reviews the application, along with the candidate's curriculum vitae, and decides whether to accept or reject it.

If the application is accepted, the candidate moves on to a job interview. This job interview consists of a meeting, where the recruiter knows more about the candidate. In an interview, a candidate can be rejected or accepted. An interview is also an opportunity to negotiate the terms of employment.

When the candidate is hired, they must sign a contract. The contract is the formal document where all the terms of the employment are established. With the signing of the contract, the candidate already has a new job. But, they must wait for a while to receive their first salary. Usually, they must wait a month before receiving their first salary.

Vocabulary

1. **empresa**	company
2. **dedica**	dedicate
3. **productiva**	productive
4. **difieren**	differ
5. **según**	according
6. **fábrica**	factory
7. **tienda**	store
8. **empleados**	employees
9. **necesario**	necessary
10. **proceso**	process
11. **generalmente**	usually
12. **oferta de trabajo**	job offer
13. **periódico**	newspaper
14. **local**	local
15. **internet**	internet
16. **oficina de empleo**	employment office
17. **disponibles**	available
18. **revisar**	check
19. **capacidades**	capacities
20. **experiencia**	experience
21. **entrenamiento**	training
22. **habilidades**	skills
23. **esenciales**	essential
24. **presentar**	present
25. **solicitud de empleo**	job application
26. **solicitud de empleo**	job application

27. **manifiesta**	manifest
28. **formalmente**	formally
29. **relevante**	relevant
30. **entrega**	delivery
31. **candidato**	candidate
32. **curriculum vitae**	curriculum vitae
33. **experiencia**	experience
34. **estudios**	studies
35. **departamento**	department
36. **recursos humanos**	human resources
37. **revisan**	check
38. **determinan**	determine
39. **cumple**	meets
40. **requisitos**	requirements
41. **rechazada**	rejected
42. **indicados**	indicated
43. **entrevista de trabajo**	job interview
44. **reclutamiento**	recruitment
45. **contratar**	contract
46. **lleva a cabo**	performed
47. **bien vestido**	well dressed
48. **copias**	copies
49. **acreditar**	accredit
50. **lista**	list
51. **rechazar**	to refuse
52. **por lo general**	as usual
53. **finalistas**	finalists
54. **lista de finalistas**	list of finalists

55. **representantes**	representatives
56. **decisión**	decision
57. **alto nivel**	high level
58. **responsabilidad**	responsibility
59. **notificado**	notified
60.**selección**	selection
61. **elabora**	elaborate
62. **contrato**	contract
63. **horario de trabajo**	working hours
64. **beneficios**	benefits
65. **términos**	terms
66. **negociar**	negotiate
67. **de acuerdo**	in agreement
68. **firma**	firm
69. **empresa privada**	private company
70. **período**	period
71. **consideración**	consideration
72. **anticipado**	anticipated
73. **situaciones**	situations
74. **durar**	to last
75. **depende**	it depends

Questions About the Story

1. ¿Qué indica una oferta de empleo?
    a. Muchos beneficios para el trabajo
    b. Muchas tareas y trabajo que hacer
    c. Las condiciones del empleo
    d. Las formas de realizar el empleo
2. ¿Qué hace una persona interesada en un empleo?
    a. Presenta su solicitud de empleo
    b. Presenta su interés por trabajar
    c. Presenta su forma de trabajar
    d. Presenta su nueva forma de vestir
3. ¿Qué es una solicitud de empleo?
    a. Es un documento muy grande
    b. Es una manifestación de interés
    c. Es un documento muy complicado
    d. Es una forma de presentarse
4. ¿Quién revisa la solicitud de empleo?
    a. La persona encargada de trabajar
    b. La persona llena de entusiasmo
    c. La persona encargada de contratación
    d. La persona que trabaja en casa
5. ¿Qué es un contrato de trabajo?
    a. Es la contratación oficial del candidato

b. Es el documento oficial de la empresa

c. Es una forma de trabajar eficientemente

d. Es la manera que se hacen las cosas

Answers

1. C
2. A
3. B
4. C
5. A

Chapter Fourteen

Festivals and Celebrations — Festivales y celebraciones

En mi país, tenemos muchas **celebraciones** y **festivales**. Algunas celebraciones son muy **coloridas**, **alegres** y **emocionantes**. Otras son más **solemnes** y **respetuosas**. Pero, de todas formas, nos **la pasamos muy bien** en familia y con amigos. Estas celebraciones hacen de nuestras vidas muy especiales.

La celebración más grande en mi país es la celebración del **Día de la Independencia**. **Cada año**, se celebra el fin de la **época colonial**. Con el fin de esta época, se da el inicio de la nueva **república**. **Típicamente**, esta celebración dura unas dos **semanas**. Las personas igual van a trabajar y a estudiar, pero se **dedica** tiempo a las celebraciones especiales.

En las escuelas, los niños celebran la independencia con **actos** en donde se **reconoce** la **historia** de nuestro país y la **diversidad** que existe en él. También se **realizan** actividades que dan **tributo** a nuestro **legado ancestral**. Los niños disfrutan este tipo de celebraciones, sobre todo porque tienen la **oportunidad** de **adornar** su escuela.

Quizá la celebración más grande es la **Navidad**. La Navidad es una celebración de origen **religioso**. Es una celebración de origen **cristiano**. Entonces, esta celebración tiene un **significado** muy importante para aquellas personas cristianas que tienen una **fe** muy **profunda**.

La Navidad también es una época de **alegría** y **felicidad**. Para muchas personas, es una **oportunidad** de hacer buenas **acciones**, ayudar a la gente **necesitada** y manifestar sus **buenos deseos**. En esta época, las reuniones con amigos y familia son muy comunes. Usualmente, las reuniones consisten en alguna comida, o bien, **asistir** a la iglesia.

Después de la Navidad, la celebración del **Año Nuevo** es muy importante. El año termina en **diciembre** y el nuevo año iniciar en enero. **Durante este tiempo**, hay muchas fiestas para **despedir** el año anterior y darle la **bienvenida** al nuevo año. **Por todas partes**, se ve alegría y felicidad. Debemos dar gracias por las cosas positivas del año anterior y estar **optimistas** para el año nuevo. La Navidad y el Año Nuevo típicamente se **celebran** en los mismos días puesto que la Navidad se celebra el veinticuatro y veinticinco de diciembre, mientras que el Año Nuevo se celebra el treinta y uno de diciembre y uno de **enero**. Estas es una época muy importante en mi país.

Luego, existen otras celebraciones muy famosas. En algunas de estas celebraciones no son **feriados nacionales**, pero sí son celebradas **ampliamente** por todas las personas en mi país.

Por ejemplo, el **Día de la Madre** es muy famoso. Este día se celebra en **mayo** en mi país. Las familias celebran este día con música, **flores** y **regalos** para las madrecitas. Muchas familias celebran este día en un restaurante o con un viaje. De igual manera, se celebra el **Día del Padre**. Este día se celebra en el mes de **junio**. La celebración es muy similar a la celebración del Día de la Madre. También existe el día de los **abuelitos**. Este día se celebra en diferentes fechas en diversos países. En mi país, esta celebración se lleva a cabo en el mes de **julio**. Es muy divertido realizar una celebración para nuestros **queridos** abuelitos.

Otro tipo de celebraciones **conmemorativas** son aquellas que reconocen algún **evento significativo** en la historia de un país. Por ejemplo, existen días que conmemoran famosas **batallas militares**, los **veteranos de guerras**, **revoluciones**, o el **nacimiento** de algún **héroe nacional**. Durante estas **ocasiones**, se llevan a cabo **ceremonias** en donde se reconoce el evento histórico. En las escuelas, los niños aprenden el significado de estos eventos.

Cuando una celebración o conmemoración es un feriado nacional, este día se declara por medio de una **ley oficial**. Usualmente, los **trabajadores** y estudiantes tienen un día libre. Esto les permite observar la celebración del feriado, o bien, simplemente pasar más tiempo en familia. Debido a que se trata de un feriado nacional, los trabajadores aun reciben su **sueldo**.

Los festivales son celebraciones **típicas** de cada país. Un festival **normalmente** es una gran **fiesta local**, o bien nacional, en donde la **cultura** y **folclor** de un país es **evidente**. Durante estas celebraciones, se observan **bailes**, comida, y **disfraces** típicos de ese país. Los festivales son excelentes oportunidades para los turistas. Cuando un **turista** visita un país durante un festival, el turista puede ver la **maravilla** de la cultura de ese país.

Resumen de la historia

Los festivales y celebraciones en mi país son variados. Existen feriados nacionales, fechas especiales y festivales. El día más importante de mi país es el Día de la Independencia. Este feriado celebra el fin de la época colonial en mi país y el inicio de la nueva república. Este feriado se observa con muchas celebraciones y actos en las escuelas.

Luego, la Navidad y el Año Nuevo son las celebraciones más famosas. La Navidad es una celebración religiosa de origen cristiano. Además de ello, las personas celebran esta ocasión en familia y con amigos. Es una época en donde se manifiestan los buenos deseos. En el caso del Año Nuevo, es una muy buena oportunidad para despedir el año anterior y dar la bienvenida al nuevo año.

Existen otras celebraciones importantes como el Día de la Madre, el Día del Padre y el Día de los Abuelitos. Estas celebraciones no son feriados oficiales en mi país, pero son de mucha importancia para todas las familias.

Además, existen otro tipo de eventos que conmemoran batallas militares, veteranos de guerra o eventos significativo en la historia de mi país. En estos casos, se realizan ceremonias para recordar estos eventos. Así mismo, hay festivales locales y nacionales en donde se celebra la cultura nacional con bailes, comida y disfraces. Estos festivales son una buena oportunidad para los turistas.

Summary of the Story

The festivals and celebrations in my country are varied. There are national holidays, special dates, and festivals. The most important day in my country is Independence Day. This holiday celebrates the end of the colonial era in my country and the beginning of the new republic. This holiday is observed with many celebrations and events in schools.

Then, Christmas and the New Year are the most famous celebrations. Christmas is a religious celebration of Christian origin. In addition, people celebrate this occasion with family and friends. It is a time where good wishes manifest. In the case of the New Year, it is a very good opportunity to say goodbye to the previous year and welcome the new year.

There are other important celebrations such as Mother's Day, Father's Day, and Grandparents' Day. These celebrations are not official holidays in my country, but they are very important for all families.

In addition, there are other types of events that commemorate military battles, war veterans, or significant events in the history of my country. In these cases, ceremonies are held to remember these events. Likewise, there are local and national festivals where national culture is celebrated with dances, food, and costumes. These festivals are a good opportunity for tourists.

Vocabulary

1. **celebraciones**	celebrations
2. **festivales**	festivals
3. **coloridas**	colorful
4. **alegres**	happy
5. **emocionantes**	exciting
6. **solemnes**	solemn
7. **respetuosas**	respectful
8. **la pasamos muy bien**	we had a great time
9. **día de la independencia**	Independence Day
10. **cada año**	every year
11. **época**	time
12. **colonial**	colonial
13. **república**	republic
14. **típicamente**	typically
15. **semanas**	weeks
16. **dedica**	dedicate
17. **actos**	acts
18. **reconoce**	recognize
19. **historia**	history
20. **diversidad**	diversity
21. **realizan**	perform
22. **tributo**	tribute
23. **legado**	legacy
24. **ancestral**	ancestral
25. **oportunidad**	opportunity
26. **adornar**	decorate

27. **quizá**	maybe
28. **navidad**	Christmas
29. **religioso**	religious
30. **cristiano**	Christian
31. **significado**	meaning
32. **fe**	faith
33. **profunda**	deep
34. **alegría**	joy
35. **felicidad**	happiness
36. **oportunidad**	opportunity
37. **acciones**	actions
38. **necesitada**	needed
39. **buenos deseos**	good wishes
40. **asistir**	assist
41. **año nuevo**	new year
42. **diciembre**	December
43. **durante este tiempo**	during this time
44. **despedir**	fire
45. **bienvenida**	welcome
46. **por todas partes**	all over
47. **optimistas**	optimistic
48. **celebran**	celebrate
49. **enero**	January
50. **feriados**	holidays
51. **nacionales**	nationals
52. **ampliamente**	widely
53. **día de la madre**	Mother's Day
54. **mayo**	may
55. **flores**	flowers

56. **regalos**	gifts
57. **día del padre**	Father's Day
58. **junio**	June
59. **abuelitos**	grandparents
60. **julio**	July
61. **queridos**	dear ones
62. **conmemorativas**	commemorative
63. **evento significativo**	significant event
64. **batallas militares**	military battles
65. **veteranos de guerras**	war veterans
66. **revoluciones**	revolutions
67. **nacimiento**	birth
68. **héroe nacional**	National hero
69. **ocasiones**	occasions
70. **ceremonias**	ceremonies
71. **ley oficial**	official law
72. **trabajadores**	workers
73. **sueldo**	salary
74. **típicas**	typical
75. **normalmente**	usually
76. **fiesta local**	local party
77. **cultura**	culture
78. **folclor**	folklore
79. **evidente**	evident
80. **bailes**	dances
81. **disfraces**	costumes
82. **turista**	tourist
83. **maravilla**	wonder

Questions About the Story

1. ¿Qué es un feriado?
    a. Es un día nuevo
    b. En un día libre
    c. Es un día malo
    d. Es un día fuerte
2. ¿Cuál es una celebración muy importante?
    a. Año viejo
    b. Año bueno
    c. Año nuevo
    d. Año feliz
3. ¿Qué es la Navidad?
    a. Es una celebración militar
    b. Es una celebración nueva
    c. Es una celebración clara
    d. Es una celebración religiosa
4. ¿Qué tipo de eventos se conmemoran?
    a. Eventos históricos
    b. Eventos novedosos
    c. Eventos sociales
    d. Eventos interesantes
5. ¿Qué se celebra en un festival?
    a. La cultura interesante

b. La cultura nacional

c. La cultura espacial

d. La cultura divertida

Answers

1. B
2. C
3. D
4. A
5. B

Chapter Fifteen

The Weather in My City — El clima de mi ciudad

Cuando las personas me **preguntan** por el **clima** en mi ciudad, siempre **desean** saber si es **cálido** o **frío**. La verdad es que el clima en mi ciudad es **templado**, es decir, no es ni frío ni cálido. La mayoría del año, la **temperatura** de mantiene entre **diez** y **veinte** grados. Esto hace del clima muy agradable. Hay días son que un poco fríos, y hay otros que son cálidos.

En el **verano**, el clima **rebasa** los treinta **grados**. Esto quiere decir que los días son muy cálidos. Es un bonito cambio porque se puede ir a la playa y disfrutar de un lindo día **soleado**. Pero, cuando hace calor por muchos días **consecutivos**, también es **desesperante**, sobre todo, en las noches. No me gusta el calor en la noche ya que es difícil **dormir** así.

En el **otoño**, el clima se pone frío y hace mucho **viento**. Los días **nublados** con comunes. También **llueve** un poco. Los **días lluvioso** de otoño son ideales para pasar en casa con un buen libro y una **taza de café**. Aunque la temperatura baja, aun se pueden hacer muchas actividades al **aire libre**. Se puede **correr**, salir en **bicicleta** y hacer deporte. El otoño es mi **estación** favorita del año.

En el **invierno**, la temperatura cae por **debajo** de los diez grados. La nieve no es usual en mi ciudad. **De hecho**, **causa** gran alegría entre los niños cuando cae nieve. Los niños juegan en sus casas, o en la escuela, cuando hay nieve. Usualmente, la nieve **tarda** dos o tres días. Son días muy alegres para todos los niños.

Cuando pasa el invierno, viene la **primavera**. Esta época de **caracteriza** por días más cálidos, pero con mucha **lluvia**. Esto es bueno porque la lluvia ayuda a **florecer** a todas las **plantas**. Los árboles se ponen verdes y crece el **césped**. Es un poco incómoda hacer ejercicio al aire libre ya que llueve bastante.

También es muy común ver a personas en la playa, **acampar en el bosque**, o simplemente practicar deportes al aire libre. Parece que la vida vuelve una vez termina el invierno. El **optimismo** vuelve a la ciudad.

Personalmente, disfruto muchísimo los días soleados, pero no muy cálidas. No me gusta el clima muy frío. **Tampoco** me gusta el clima nublado y **brumoso**. Cuando hay bruma, es difícil ver. Además, el día luce triste. Me gusta cuando el día luce alegre y con mucho optimismo.

Tenemos una playa muy grande cerca de mi ciudad. Debemos **andar** unas dos horas en auto para **llegar** a la playa. Está bien porque podemos ir y **regresar** en el mismo día. Es divertido pasar tiempo en la playa. La temperatura es un poco más cálida en la playa. Aunque, sí hace frío en el invierno. Tengo amigos que les gusta la playa en invierno. Es divertido porque puedes **apreciar** el **mar** y caminar sobre la **arena**. Pero el agua está muy fría. Entonces, no es buena idea **meterse** en el agua a nadar.

Y tú, ¿cómo es el clima en tu ciudad? ¿Cómo es en tu país? ¿Vives es un país cálido o frío?

Si vives en un país cálido, seguramente tienes buen clima todo el año. No debes **preocuparte** por el frío o la nieve. Si vives en un país frío, creo que debes tener cuidado con el invierno. Lo mejor de cada estación del año es que puedes hacer diferentes actividades. Cuando hay nieve, puedes hacer actividades del invierno. Por ejemplo, **patinar sobe hielo** es muy divertido.

La única época en donde no puedes hacer mucho es durante la época lluviosa. En esta época debes permanecer adentro. La lluvia no te permite hacer mucho. **A menos** que disfrutes correr bajo el agua, realmente no se puede hacer mucho cuando llueve fuerte. Estos días son para **permanecer** en casa, viendo televisión, o bien, **leyendo un buen libro**.

Todos los países tienen un clima diferente. Por eso debes disfrutar el clima de tu país, o tu ciudad, al **máximo**. Seguramente conoces muchas actividades divertidas por hacer. Si algún día visito tu país, espero disfrutarlo de la misma manera que tú lo haces. Creo que eso **será** una linda experiencia para mí, y para todos.

Resumen de la historia

El clima en mi ciudad no es cálido ni frío. El clima es templado. La temperatura se mantiene entre diez y veinte grados. Por lo regular, hace buen clima. Hay días soleados y algunos días nublados. Puedo hacer muchas actividades al aire libre especialmente durante el verano y el otoño.

En mi país, se observan las cuatro estaciones, invierno, primavera, verano y otoño. Mi estación favorita es el otoño. Disfruto el verano, pero no me gusta cuando hace mucho calor en el verano porque no puedo dormir en las noches. Lo mejor del verano y es ir a la playa que está cerca de mi ciudad.

En el invierno hace un poco de frío. También cae nieve, aunque no es mucha. Los niños son felices cuando hay nieve porque pueden jugar en sus casas o en la escuela. La nieve dura unos dos o tres días. Esto hace muy felices a los niños.

En la primavera llueve mucho. Esto es bueno para las plantas, pero no me gusta porque no puedo hacer muchas cosas al aire libre. Los días nublados y lluviosos son buenos para estar en casa, ver la televisión y leer un buen libro. Los días lluviosos y brumosos lucen muy tristes.

Summary of the Story

The weather in my city is neither hot nor cold. The weather is warm. The temperature usually stays between ten and twenty degrees. It usually has good weather. There are sunny days and some cloudy days. I can do many outdoor activities, especially during summer and fall.

In my country, the four seasons are can be seen—winter, spring, summer, and autumn. My favorite season is autumn. I enjoy summer, but I don't like it when it is very hot in the summer because I can't sleep at night. The best thing about summer is going to the beach that is close to my city.

In the winter, it is a bit cold. Snow also falls, although it is not much. Children are happy when there is snow because they can play at home or at school. The snow lasts about two or three days. This makes the children very happy.

In the spring, it rains a lot. This is good for plants, but I don't like it because I can't do many things outdoors. Cloudy and rainy days are good for being at home, watching TV, and reading a good book. Rainy and foggy days look very sad.

Vocabulary

1. **preguntan**	they ask
2. **clima**	weather
3. **desean**	wish
4. **cálido**	warm
5. **frío**	cold
6. **templado**	temperate
7. **temperatura**	temperature
8. **diez**	ten
9. **veinte**	twenty
10. **verano**	summer
11. **rebasa**	exceeds
12. **grados**	degrees
13. **soleado**	sunny
14. **consecutivos**	consecutive
15. **desesperante**	maddening
16. **dormir**	sleep
17. **otoño**	autumn
18. **viento**	wind
19. **nublados**	overcast
20. **llueve**	rains
21. **días lluvioso**	rainy days
22. **taza de café**	cup of coffee
23. **aire libre**	fresh air
24. **correr**	run
25. **bicicleta**	bike
26. **estación**	station
27. **invierno**	winter

28. **debajo**	under
29. **de hecho**	in fact
30. **causa**	cause
31. **tarda**	it takes
32. **primavera**	spring
33. **caracteriza**	characterizes
34. **lluvia**	rain
35. **florecer**	to flourish
36. **plantas**	plants
37. **césped**	grass
38. **acampar en el bosque**	camp in the woods
39. **optimismo**	optimism
40. **tampoco**	neither
41. **brumoso**	misty
42. **andar**	walk
43. **llegar**	reach
44. **regresar**	to return
45. **apreciar**	to appreciate
46. **mar**	sea
47. **arena**	sand
48. **meterse**	get in
49. **preocuparte**	worry you
50. **patinar sobe hielo**	ice skating
51. **a menos**	unless
52. **permanecer**	stay
53. **leyendo un buen libro**	reading a good book
54. **máximo**	maximum
55. **será**	will be

Questions About the Story

1. ¿Cómo es el clima de mi ciudad?
    a. Ni frío, ni caliente
    b. Extremadamente frío
    c. Muy cálido en verano
    d. No es muy cálidos
2. ¿Cuál es mi estación favorita?
    a. La estación del tren
    b. La estación de radio
    c. El otoño
    d. La primavera
3. ¿Por qué son malos los días lluviosos?
    a. Porque se destruye la ciudad
    b. Porque se compran autos
    c. Porque no puedo comer nada
    d. Porque no puedo salir a jugar
4. ¿Qué pasa en el invierno?
    a. Los niños juegan afuera
    b. Los adultos no trabajan
    c. Hace frío y cae nieve
    d. No hace calor ni lluvia
5. ¿Qué pasa con los niños cuando neva?
    a. Los niños juegan afuera

b. Los adultos no trabajan

c. Hace frío y cae nieve

d. No hace calor ni lluvia

Answers

1. A
2. C
3. D
4. C
5. A

Chapter Sixteen

My Favorite Colors — Mis colores favoritos

La vida está **llena** de colores. Algunos colores son más **fuertes** que otros. Otros colores son más **oscuros**. Algunos otros son más alegres. Otros son más **discretos**. En realidad, la vida está llena de toda clase de **tonalidades** y de **sombras**. Sin los colores, la vida sería muy **aburrida** y sin sentido.

De todos los colores en el mundo, es difícil **escoger** solo uno. Muchas personas me preguntan: ¿cuál es tu color favorito? Pero es muy difícil escoger solo uno. **Quizá** una mejor pregunta sería, ¿cuáles son **tus** colores favoritos? A esa pregunta sí tengo una **respuesta**.

Primero, uno de mis colores favoritos es el **azul**. Este color lo puedo combinar con mi **ropa**, mis **zapatos**, y prácticamente cualquier otra cosa. Mi auto es azul. Pero, mi casa es celeste. **Celeste** es una tonalidad de azul, es mucho más claro que el azul. De hecho, se dice que el **cielo** es celeste. Es un color hermoso que representa mucha **paz** y **libertad**.

Luego, otro de los colores que me encanta es el **verde**. El verde me inspira mucha **tranquilidad**. **Creo** que es un color que va con cualquier cosa. Se ve bien en la ropa, en una casa, en un auto y, **por supuesto**, en la comida. El verde representa tantas cosas a la vez. Existen muchas tonalidades de verde, pero creo que la tonalidad que mejor me representa es el **verde olivo**. Es un color muy bonito.

Así mismo, uno de los colores que tanto me gusta es el **marrón**. Algunas personas también le llaman "café". El marrón es un color **neutro**, es decir, no es el tipo de color que **resalta**. Es un color que **sirve** de **base** para **combinarse** con otros colores. Por ejemplo, puedes usar **pantalones** marrones con una **chaqueta** azul. Esta combinación se ve bien, es **elegante**, se puede usar tanto en una situación formal como en una situación casual.

Otro de los colores que me **fascina** es el **blanco**. El color blanco no es muy popular porque es muy delicado. Cuando se dice que es delicado, es porque fácilmente se **ensucia** o se **mancha**. Pero es un color muy elegante. Me gustan mucho las **camisetas** blancas. Aunque no me gustan las **medias** blancas, sí me parece genial usar una camiseta blanca con **vaqueros** oscuros. Creo que esta es una muy buena combinación en cualquier lugar que vaya.

Finalmente, creo que el color que más uso en mi ropa es el negro. Muchas personas no usan el color negro porque lo **asocian** con el **duelo**, es decir, cuando una persona muere. Es cierto, se usa este color cuando una persona ha **muerto**. Pero en realidad, es un color muy elegante si se usa adecuadamente. Tengo pantalones, vaqueros y chaquetas negras. Esta ropa se ve bien en **cualquier** ocasión. El único problema con el color negro es cuando hace mucho calor. El color negro siempre **absorbe** más calor.

Mis colores favoritos no son los únicos colores que existen. Por ejemplo, está el **rosa**. El color rosa es usualmente asociado con un toque femenino. Si bien los hombres también pueden usar este color, es mucho más común **verlo** en las mujeres.

Estos son algunos colores que también son populares: **gris**, **rojo**, **amarillo**, **morado** y **naranja**. Todos estos colores se ven por todas partes. El color muchas veces depende del artículo. En el caso de los autos, los autos amarillos y rojos son más exóticos. Pero, el rojo no es un color usado para **pintar** una casa. Una habitación usualmente es pintada de blanco, o un color claro como celeste o un verde **claro**.

En definitiva, la vida es mucho más bonita cuando está llena de colores. No importa cuál es tu color favorito. Lo que importa es que uses el color que más te gusta. Cuando usas colores que te gustan, **sientes** la vida mucho más alegre. Sin estos colores, la vida es más triste. Personalmente, mis colores favoritos siempre me **motivan** a trabajar, estudiar, o simplemente pasarla bien. En mi casa, tengo todos los colores que más me gustan. De esa manera, **me puedo** sentir **a gusto** en mi casa. Puedo sentir la **comodidad** de tener el espacio que a mí me gusta tanto.

Resumen de la historia

La vida está llena de colores. No puedo escoger un solo color ya que me gustan todos los colores. Pero, en particular, hay algunos colores que me hacen sentir mejor que otros. El color que más me gusta usar es el azul. Mi ropa y mi auto son de color azul. Creo que la tonalidad más bonita del azul es el celeste. El cielo es celeste.

Otros colores que me gustan son el verde. El verde olivo es mi tonalidad favorita. El verde es un color que se puede utilizar en cualquier situación. Me da mucha tranquilidad usar verde. El marrón, también conocido como café, es uno de los colores que más me gustan. Es un color neutro y se puede combinar con muchos otros colores.

El blanco es un color que tanto me gusta. Aunque el blanco se puede manchar fácilmente, es un color que va con cualquier ropa. De igual manera, me gusta mucho usar el negro. Muchas personas piensan que el color negro es muy triste porque se usa cuando una persona muere. Pero creo que es un color elegante.

Otros colores que se pueden usar son el rojo, amarillo, morado, naranja y gris. Estos colores son populares y se pueden ver en todas partes.

Summary of the Story

Life is full of colors. I cannot choose a single color since I like all the colors. But in particular, there are some colors that make me feel better than others. The color I like to wear the most is blue. My clothes and car are blue. I think the prettiest shade of blue is light blue. The sky is light blue.

Another color that I like is green. Olive green is my favorite hue. Green is a color that can be used in any situation. It gives me a lot of peace to wear green. Brown, also known as "coffee," is one of the colors that I like the most. It is a neutral color and can be combined with many other colors.

White is a color that I like so much. Although white can be easily stained, it is a color that goes with any clothing. Similarly, I really like to wear black. Many people think that black is very sad because it is used when a person dies. But I think it is an elegant color.

Other colors that can be used are red, yellow, purple, orange, and gray. These colors are popular and can be seen everywhere.

Vocabulary

1. **llena** full
2. **fuertes** strong
3. **oscuros** dark
4. **discretos** discreet
5. **tonalidades** hues
6. **sombras** shades
7. **aburrida** boring
8. **escoger** choose
9. **quizá** maybe
10. **tus** your
11. **respuesta** answer
12. **azul** blue
13. **ropa** clothing
14. **zapatos** shoes
15. **celeste** light blue
16. **cielo** sky
17. **paz** peace
18. **libertad** freedom
19. **verde** green
20. **tranquilidad** tranquility
21. **creo** I think
22. **por supuesto** of course
23. **verde olivo** olive green
24. **marrón** brown
25. **neutro** neutral
26. **resalta** stand out
27. **sirve** it serves

28. **base**	base
29. **combinarse**	combine
30. **pantalones**	pants
31. **chaqueta**	jacket
32. **elegante**	elegant
33. **fascina**	fascinates
34. **blanco**	white
35. **ensucia**	dirty
36. **mancha**	stain
37. **camisetas**	t-shirts
38. **medias**	socks
39. **vaqueros**	jeans
40. **asocian**	associate
41. **duelo**	duel
42. **muerto**	dead
43. **cualquier**	any
44. **absorbe**	absorbs
45. **rosa**	pink
46. **verlo**	see him
47. **gris**	gray
48. **rojo**	red
49. **amarillo**	yellow
50. **morado**	purple
51. **naranja**	orange
52. **pintar**	paint
53. **claro**	clear
54. **sientes**	you feel
55. **motivan**	motivate
56. **me puedo**	I can

57. **a gusto**	satisfied
58. **comodidad**	comfort

Questions About the Story

1. ¿Cuál es mi color favorito?
    a. El azul
    b. El rojo
    c. No tengo
    d. No quiero
2. ¿Qué color es mi auto?
    a. Amarillo
    b. Verde
    c. Rojo
    d. Azul
3. ¿Qué pasa con el color blanco?
    a. Se cambia difícilmente
    b. Se mancha fácilmente
    c. Se vuelve ampliamente
    d. Se desarrolla rápidamente
4. ¿Por qué es triste el negro?
    a. Se usa cuando hay problemas
    b. Se usa cuando hay desastres
    c. Se usa cuando una persona muere
    d. Se usa cuando no se sabe que hacer
5. ¿Por qué es bonito el marrón?
    a. Tiene varias tonalidades

b. Se puede combinar con todo

c. No se entiende el color

d. Es importante hacer algo

Answers

1. C
2. D
3. B
4. C
5. B

Chapter Seventeen

My Best Friends — Mis mejores amigos

Soy muy **afortunada** de tener amigos tan maravillosos. Tengo muchos amigos por todas **partes**: en el trabajo, en mi **vecindario**, en la universidad y en el gimnasio. Todos mis amigos son amables, **serviciales** y atentos conmigo. **Frecuentemente**, salimos a comer, vamos al cine o tenemos una reunión para cenar. Todos mis amigos tienen **cualidades** que los hace **excepcionales**.

Aunque es cierto que tengo muchos amigos, solamente tengo tres amigos que considero mis mejores amigos.

Primero, está Pamela. Tengo muchos años de ser amiga de Pamela. Nos conocemos desde hace muchos años. Pamela y yo tenemos la misma edad... **veintisiete** años. Ella es una chica tan **linda**. Ella es amable, **cariñosa** y siempre está dispuesta a ayudarme cuando tengo algún problema. Con ella, nunca tenemos **discusiones** ni **peleas**. Cuando tenemos alguna **diferencia de opinión**, siempre encontramos alguna manera de resolver nuestras diferencias.

Pamela es alta, **atlética** y muy dedicada a su trabajo. Ella trabaja como **diseñadora** para una empresa de **construcción**. Es **verdaderamente** muy talentosa. Sus diseños son increíbles. Realmente tiene muy buen gusto para la decoración. Nos llevamos muy bien porque vamos juntas al gimnasio **prácticamente** todos los días.

Luego, está Javier. Javier es un chico muy especial. Tiene veintiséis años. Él es un **compañero** de la universidad. Tenemos tres años de conocernos. En este tiempo se ha convertido en uno de mis mejores amigos. Se puede decir que **hacemos** "clic". Él es amable y muy cariñoso. Pero también es fuerte y decidido. Él también es muy protector. Siempre que salimos, él se asegura de que nada nos pase.

No cabe duda de que Javier es un chico muy alegre. Siempre cuenta chistes y les encuentra el lado positivo a las cosas. En definitiva, **nos llevamos muy bien**. Me encanta su forma tan optimista de ver la vida. Creo que somos muy **parecidos**.

Mi otra mejor amiga es Carla. Carla es una compañera de trabajo. Con ella, tenemos más de cuatro años de trabajar juntas. Nos conocemos muy bien. Ella y yo trabajamos en el mismo departamento, pero hacemos trabajos diferentes. Ella es **contadora** y yo estoy encargada de **gestionar** las compras de la empresa. En muchas ocasiones, tenemos que trabajar juntas. Incluso, tenemos que viajar para visitar **clientes** y **proveedores**.

Carla es una chica **extraordinaria**. Ella tiene veinticuatro años, pero **actúa** muy madura para su edad. Siempre tiene un consejo muy útil para cualquier situación. Yo sé que puedo contar con ella cuando tengo un problema. Ella siempre tiene una buena idea que podemos poner en práctica. Ella es muy **inteligente** y **analítica**. Creo que estas dos cualidades son muy importantes para el trabajo que ella realiza.

Pamela, Javier y Carla son mis mejores amigos. Sé que puedo contar con ellos cuando tengo necesidad de un **consejo**, el apoyo de un amigo, o simplemente alguien para escuchar. Pero no siempre el apoyo es para mí. Yo estoy feliz de apoyarlos cuando ellos me necesitan. Cuando ellos tienen necesidad de mí, saben que pueden contar conmigo. Ellos saben que tienen una amiga **incondicional** en mí.

Le tengo mucho aprecio y cariño a todos mis amigos. No sé qué **haría** sin mis amigos. Pero mis mejores amigos son mi **fuerza**. Ellos me **acompañan** cuando más necesito a un amigo. A menudo, los cuatro nos apoyamos. No importa quien tiene necesidad de ayuda; siempre estamos ahí para darnos apoyo, cariño y buenos consejos.

Y cuando se trata de pasarla bien... ¡también estamos ahí! Pronto, nos **iremos** de vacaciones. Yo quiero ir a la playa a pasar unos días bajo el sol. Javier quiere ir a practicar **montañismo**. Y, Pamela y Carla simplemente quieren pasarla bien.

Creo que ya tenemos buenos planes para nuestras vacaciones. La vamos a pasar muy bien. Estoy segura de que nuestras vacaciones serán alucinantes. Vamos a pasarla de maravilla.

¿Quiénes son tus mejores amigos? Si tus amigos son tan especiales como los míos, entonces eres una persona muy afortunada. Cuida mucho de tus amigos. Los amigos son mucho más valiosos que cualquier otra cosa en la vida.

Resumen de la historia

Tengo muchos amigos. Tengo amigos en el trabajo, la universidad y el gimnasio. Todos mis amigos son muy especiales conmigo. Siempre tengo amigos con quienes salir, ir al cine y pasarla bien. Todos mis amigos son excepcionales.

Pero mis mejores amigos son Pamela, Javier y Carla.

Tengo muchos años de conocer a Pamela. Ella es muy atlética y tiene la misma edad que yo... veintisiete años. Vamos juntas al gimnasio. Nos gusta hacer ejercicio. Ella es una chica muy linda. Por eso es que ella es mi mejor amiga.

Javier es mi mejor amigo de la universidad. Tenemos tres años de estudiar juntos. Él tiene veintiséis años. Es un chico muy amable, pero también es muy protector. Él siempre se dedica a cuidarnos cuando salimos juntos. Es divertido y muy optimista.

Luego, Carla es mi mejor amiga en el trabajo. Trabajamos en el mismo departamento juntas. Ella es contadora y yo soy la encargada de las compras de la empresa. Algunas veces, debemos viajar juntas por trabajo.

Mis amigos son increíbles, pero yo también soy lo mejor para ellos. Hago mi mejor esfuerzo por ser una amiga, apoyo y ayudarles todas las veces que lo necesitan. Soy muy afortunada de tener amigos tan maravillosos.

Summary of the Story

I have many friends. I have friends at work, university, and the gym. All my friends are very special to me. I always have friends with whom I go out, go to the movies, and have a good time. All my friends are exceptional.

But my best friends are Pamela, Javier, and Carla.

I have known Pamela for many years. She is very athletic and is the same age as me—twenty-seven years old. We go to the gym together. We like to exercise. She is a very pretty girl. That's why she is my best friend.

Javier is my best friend from the university. We have been studying together for three years. He is twenty-six years old. He is a very kind boy, but he is also very protective. He always takes care of us when we go out together. It is fun and very optimistic.

Then, Carla is my best friend at work. We work in the same department together. She is an accountant, and I am in charge of the company's purchases. Sometimes, we must travel together for work.

My friends are amazing, but I am also the best for them. I do my best to be a friend, support and help them all the times they need it. I am very lucky to have such wonderful friends.

Vocabulary

1. **afortunada**	lucky
2. **partes**	parts
3. **vecindario**	neighborhood
4. **serviciales**	helpful
5. **Frecuentemente**	frequently
6. **cualidades**	qualities
7. **excepcionales**	exceptional
8. **veintisiete**	twenty-seven
9. **linda**	cute
10. **cariñosa**	loving
11. **discusiones**	discussions
12. **peleas**	fights
13. **diferencia de opinión**	difference of opinion
14. **atlética**	athletic
15. **diseñadora**	designer
16. **construcción**	building
17. **verdaderamente**	truly
18. **prácticamente**	practically
19. **compañero**	companion
20. **hacemos**	we make
21. **nos llevamos muy bien**	we get along really good
22. **parecidos**	similar
23. **contadora**	accountant
24. **gestionar**	manage
25. **clientes**	customers
26. **proveedores**	suppliers

27. **extraordinaria**	extraordinary
28. **actúa**	act
29. **inteligente**	smart
30. **analítica**	analytics
31. **consejo**	advice
32. **incondicional**	unconditional
33. **haría**	would do
34. **fuerza**	strength
35. **acompañan**	accompany
36. **iremos**	we'll go
37. **montañismo**	mountaineering

Questions About the Story

1. ¿Cuántos mejores amigos tengo?
    a. Uno
    b. Dos
    c. Tres
    d. Cuatro
2. ¿Quiénes son mis mejores amigos?
    a. Javier y Claudia
    b. Javier y Pamela
    c. Pamela y Carolina
    d. Pamela y José
3. ¿Cuánto tiempo tengo de conocer a Pamela?
    a. Muchos años
    b. Pocos días
    c. Algún tiempo
    d. Hace meses
4. ¿Cuántos años tiene Javier?
    a. Veinticuatro
    b. Veinticinco
    c. Veintiséis
    d. Veintisiete
5. ¿Qué hago por mis amigos?
    a. Soy amable y cariñosa

b. Soy fuerte y agresiva

c. Soy interesante y buena

d. Soy amigable y corriente

Answers

1. C
2. B
3. A
4. C
5. A

Chapter Eighteen

When Is Your Birthday? — ¿Cuándo es tu cumpleaños?

Nuestro **cumpleaños** es el día en que **nacemos**. Para algunas personas, es un día muy especial. Este día está lleno de celebraciones, **regalos** y tiempo con familia y amigos. Esto hace de los cumpleaños una ocasión muy especial que **ocurre** cada año. Para otras personas, un cumpleaños es una ocasión más **sencilla**. No les gusta celebrar su cumpleaños porque cada año cumplen más y más años... pero de igual manera, es un día muy especial para todas las personas.

El cumpleaños se da una vez cada año. Esta celebración ocurre en uno de los meses del año. Los meses son **enero**, **febrero**, **marzo**, **abril**, **mayo**, **junio**, **julio**, **agosto**, **septiembre**, **octubre**, **noviembre** y **diciembre**. Dependiendo el mes de **nacimiento**, ese será el mes del cumpleaños. Así mismo, una persona nace en un día del mes. Unos meses tienen **treinta** días y otros tienen **treinta y un** días. Solo el mes de febrero es especial porque tiene **veintiocho** días.

Una celebración de cumpleaños típicamente es una fiesta. Esta fiesta puede ser muy grande con muchos **invitados**, música y regalos, o puede ser una fiesta más pequeña con algunos invitados y poca comida. De igual manera, el **cumpleañero** recibe toda la atención de sus amigos, familia e invitados. Es América, es costumbre dar un regalo al cumpleañero en su fiesta. Regularmente, este regalo es un artículo que se le gusta al cumpleañero o quizá algo de **utilidad**.

Un elemento **sumamente** importante que no puede faltar en una celebración de cumpleaños es el pastel. El **pastel** es lo más importante en una celebración de cumpleaños. Cuando el cumpleañero recibe su pastel, debe **apagar las velas**. Cuando apaga las velas, debe **pedir un deseo**. Pero, es importante no decir el deseo ya que si dice cual es el deseo, éste no se cumplirá.

En el pastel se coloca una vela por cada año que cumple el cumpleañero. Pero, si cumple muchos años, entonces se colocan unas cuantas velas nada más. Algunas personas **colocan** velas con los números de la edad del cumpleañero. Es una manera más práctica de **representar** la **edad** del cumpleañero. Hay algunos cumpleañeros que no les gusta decir su edad.

Para los niños, las celebraciones de cumpleaños son muy especiales. En muchos países de Latinoamérica, se acostumbra a romper una **piñata**. Una piñata es un objeto que tiene forma de algún **animal**, o bien, un **superhéroe** o cualquier otro objeto. Las piñatas están llenas de dulces o juguetitos. Luego, el cumpleañero pasa al frente a romper la piñata. Esto lo hace con un **palo de madera**. El cumpleañero debe **pegarle** a la piñata hasta romperla. De ahí, todos los niños corren a recoger los dulces. Usualmente, todos los niños presentes en la fiesta de cumpleaños tienen una oportunidad de romper la piñata. Los niños más pequeños van primero y los más grandes van de último.

Las piñatas no se **acostumbran** en las celebraciones de adultos. Cuando es una celebración de adultos, es costumbre beber un trago de alguna **bebida alcohólica** para **brindar** en **honor** al cumpleañero. La bebida más común para brindar es la champaña. La **champaña** se bebe después de decir "¡salud!" También es costumbre que el mejor amigo, o un familiar cercano, diga unas palabras especiales antes de brindar. Usualmente, estas palabras incluyen **buenos deseos** para el cumpleañero.

En cuanto a regalos, es usual regalar juguetes o ropa para un niño. Muchas personas prefieren regalar un libro o un **rompecabezas** a los niños. Estas personas creen que es mejor un regalo educativo que un juguete. Esto ayudará al niño en la escuela o a aprender cosas nuevas.

Para un adulto, los regalos dependen del tipo de relación. Por ejemplo, entre amigos es usual darse regalos como ropa, **gorras**, lentes, **relojes** o libros. De un padre hacia un hijo, es costumbre regalar algo que el padre sabe que le gusta a su hijo o hija. De igual manera, un hijo le puede dar a su padre un regalo que le gusta. Para una madre, las flores son muy comunes además de un regalo como ropa, perfume o joyas.

Cuando alguien no sabe que regalar a un amigo, hermano o quizá a un compañero de trabajo, existe la **opción** conocida como un **certificado de regalo**. Un certificado de regalo es un documento que es válido por una cantidad de dinero. Esta cantidad de dinero se puede **canjear** en una tienda específica, o bien, para compras en línea. Con esto, el cumpleañero puede comprar lo que quiere.

En conclusión, el cumpleaños de una persona es una ocasión muy especial. En definitiva, es difícil encontrar el regalo **perfecto** más no es imposible. Pero con esfuerzo y un poco de inteligencia, se puede encontrar una buena opción para agradar al cumpleañero. Solamente es cuestión de investigar un poco.

Resumen de la historia

Cuando una persona cumple años, se acostumbra a realizar una celebración especial para celebrar la ocasión. Se cumple años solamente una vez al año, es por ello que esta ocasión es especial para todas las personas. Algunas personas les gusta celebrar en grande mientras que otras personas prefieren celebrar un poco más tranquilamente.

Cuando la celebración es para un niño, se acostumbra a hacer una fiesta con un gran pastel y una piñata. Las piñatas están usualmente llenas de dulces. Pero, también pueden contener juguetitos. El cumpleañero debe romper la piñata y los demás niños recogen los dulces. Todos los niños tienen una oportunidad de romper la piñata.

En el caso de fiestas para adultos, es común celebrar con alguna bebida alcohólica. Comúnmente, se consume champaña para brindar a la salud del cumpleañero. En el momento de brindar, una persona muy especial en la vida del cumpleañero dice algunas palabras especiales para la ocasión. Luego, todos dicen "¡salud!" y beben.

Otra tradición es apagar las velas. Cuando el cumpleañero apaga las velas, debe pedir un deseo. Pero, debe tener cuidado de no decir el deseo. De lo contrario, no se cumplirá. Otra parte de un cumpleaños es elegir el regalo perfecto. Los regalos dependen de la persona. Si el cumpleañero es un niño, se acostumbra a regalar un juguete o un libro. Si es un adulto, los regalos pueden variar. Algunas personas prefieren regalar un certificado de regalo. De esa cuenta, el cumpleañero puede comprar cualquier cosa que le gusta.

Summary of the Story

When it is a person's birthday, it is customary to hold a special celebration to celebrate the occasion. It is a person's birthday only once a year; that is why this occasion is special for all people. Some people like to celebrate big, while other people prefer to celebrate a little more quietly.

When the celebration is for a child, it is customary to have a party with a big cake and a piñata. Piñatas are usually full of candy. But, they can also contain toys. The birthday boy or girl must break the piñata, and the other children collect the candy. All children have a chance to break the piñata.

In the case of parties for adults, it is common to celebrate with an alcoholic beverage. Commonly, champagne is consumed to provide good wishes to the birthday boy or girl. At the time of toasting, a very special person in the birthday boy or girl's life says some special words for the occasion. Then everyone says "cheers!" and they drink.

Another tradition is to blow out the candles. When the birthday boy or girl blows out the candles, they must make a wish. But, they must be careful not to say the wish. Otherwise, it will not come true. Another part of a birthday celebration is choosing the perfect gift. Gifts depend on the person. If the occasion is for a child, they usually get a toy or a book as a present. If it is an adult, gifts may vary. Some people prefer to give a gift certificate. In that case, the birthday boy or girl can buy anything they like.

Vocabulary

1. **cumpleaños** birthday
2. **nacemos** we are born
3. **regalos** gifts
4. **ocurre** it happens
5. **sencilla** simple
6. **enero** January
7. **febrero** February
8. **marzo** March
9. **abril** April
10. **mayo** may
11. **junio** June
12. **julio** July
13. **agosto** August
14. **septiembre** September
15. **octubre** October
16. **noviembre** November
17. **diciembre** December
18. **nacimiento** birth
19. **treinta** thirty
20. **treinta y un** thirty-one
21. **veintiocho** twenty-eight
22. **invitados** guests
23. **cumpleañero** birthday boy
24. **utilidad** utility
25. **sumamente** extremely
26. **pastel** cake
27. **apagar las velas** blow out the candles

28. **pedir un deseo**	make a wish
29. **colocan**	place
30. **representar**	represent
31. **edad**	age
32. **piñata**	piñata
33. **animal**	animal
34. **superhéroe**	super hero
35. **palo de madera**	wooden stick
36. **pegarle**	hit him
37. **acostumbran**	get used
38. **bebida alcohólica**	alcoholic beverage
39. **brindar**	toast
40. **honor**	honor
41. **champaña**	champagne
42. **buenos deseos**	good wishes
43. **rompecabezas**	puzzle
44. **gorras**	hats
45. **relojes**	watches
46. **opción**	option
47. **certificado de regalo**	gift certificate
48. **canjear**	exchange
49. **perfecto**	perfect

Questions About the Story

1. ¿Por qué es especial un cumpleaños?
    a. Porque es un día libre siempre
    b. Porque es el día que nacemos
    c. Porque es el día de mis amigos
    d. Porque es un día sin trabajo
2. ¿Cuándo es tu cumpleaños?
    a. Todos los meses
    b. Cada fin de semana
    c. Una vez al año
    d. Cada dos años
3. ¿De qué está llena una piñata?
    a. Comida
    b. Carritos
    c. Divertido
    d. Dulces
4. ¿Qué se dice a la hora de brindar?
    a. Bueno
    b. Suerte
    c. Amor
    d. Salud
5. ¿Cuál es una tradición de cumpleaños?
    a. Apagar las velas

b. Apagar el pastel

c. Apagar la comida

d. Apagar los regalos

Answers

1. B
2. C
3. D
4. D
5. A

Chapter Nineteen

The Best Family in the World — La mejor familia del mundo

Tengo la **mejor** familia del mundo. Mi familia no es muy grande; **de hecho**, es **relativamente** pequeña. Pero **no cabe duda** de que es la mejor familia de todas. Yo **sé** que todas las familias son especiales, pero la mía es mejor que cualquierotra.

¿**Porqué**?

Buena pregunta.

Para empezar, somos cinco personas en mi familia. Está mi **padre**, Guillermo. Él es médico. Él trabaja en un hospital. Su trabajo es muy fuerte. Siempre está **atendiendo** personas enfermas o heridas. Es muy bueno en su trabajo. Por eso es que las personas lo buscan cuando necesitan ayuda. Muchas veces, trabaja noches y fines de semana. Él es muy **dedicado** a su trabajo.

Pero también es una persona muy **alegre** y **divertida**. Él siempre tiene algo interesante que contar. Con respecto a alguna característica **negativa**, puedo decir que mi padre es **estricto** y **exigente**. Siempre nos dice a mis hermanos y a mí que debemos ser buenos estudiantes. Nos exige buenas notas en nuestros exámenes. A veces es un poco molesto, pero sé que lo hace por nuestro bien.

Luego, está mi **madre**, Sofía. Ella es muy **tierna** y **cariñosa**. Siempre nos cuida y consiente cuando estamos mal o tenemos algún problema. Ella no nos deja **sufrir**. Siempre busca la mejor manera de **hacernos sentir mejor**. Ella trabaja en una empresa como gerente de recursos humanos. Tiene un trabajo menos exigente que el de mi padre.

Mi madre también es estricta. Ella espera lo mejor de nosotros. Estamos **conscientes** de que ella nos exige **buen comportamiento** porque es lo mejor para nosotros. Nos habla y nos dice cosas positivas. Siempre que tenemos alguna dificultad, ella nos da ánimo para seguir adelante.

De ahí, están mis hermanos. Mi hermano mayor, Carlos, es **deportista**. Él tiene dieciséis años y juega en el equipo de basquetbol de mi escuela. También juega tenis los fines de semana. Yo creo que le gusta más el tenis que el basquetbol. También es muy popular en la escuela. Tiene muchos amigos. Además, es muy popular con las chicas. Todo el mundo quiere estar **cerca** de él.

Al igual que sus **cualidades** positivas, también tiene cualidades negativas. Algunas veces puede ser **brusco**, es decir, me **empuja** o me **grita**. Yo sé que me quiere y jamás me **lastimaría**. Creo que esa es simplemente la relación normal entre hermanos.

Mi hermana, Laura, es muy **bonita**. Es una chica super inteligente. Siempre saca las mejores notas de su clase. Tiene quince años. Todos los chicos la buscan porque no sólo es linda, sino que también sabe mucho **sobre** muchas cosas. Además, es amigable y tiene una sonrisa muy **contagiosa**. Ella nunca está enojada ni triste. Es muy alegre, jovial y amable. Tiene muchas amigas que siempre la siguen por todas partes.

Es difícil encontrar algo negativo sobre mi hermana. Pero, a veces es terca. Cuando ella decide que algo se hará a su manera, es muy difícil hacerla **cambiar de parecer**. Por una parte, es una buena cualidad ya que **nadie** juega con ella, pero al mismo tiempo, es difícil **razonar** con ella. De todas formas, la amo porque es mi hermana.

Finalmente, estoy yo. Tengo doce años y soy estudiante. Me encanta estudiar. Soy muy feliz cuando estudio matemáticas y ciencias. Soy aficionado a las **estrellas**. Por eso me gusta la **astronomía**. Creo que es una ciencia muy interesante. **Me gustaría** ser **astrofísico** algún día. Hay mucho que aprender.

Pero, también me gustan los deportes. Mi deporte favorito es el béisbol. También me gusta el basquetbol, pero no soy tan alto como mi hermano. Todo el mundo me dice que pronto seré del mismo **tamaño** de mi hermano. Quizá es cierto. Pero no quiero ser como mi hermano; quiero ser yo mismo.

Somos cinco en total en mi familia. Pero hay más **miembros** de mi familia. Están mis **tíos**. Tengo dos tíos y cuatro **tías**. Además, tengo nueve **primos**. Y también están mis cuatro abuelitos. Mis dos abuelas son lindas conmigo. Mis dos abuelos son muy cariñosos. Siempre me están dando consejos para el estudio y el deporte.

Al final de cuentas tengo una familia grande. Cuando hay una **reunión**, toda la familia se junta en una casa. Usualmente, es en casa de uno de mis abuelitos. La familia se ve grande, hay mucha comida, y mucha diversión entre todos los primos.

Creo que tenemos una familia muy especial. Soy afortunado de vivir en una familia en donde todos nos **queremos** y nos **apoyamos**. Es verdaderamente la mejor familia en el mundo.

Resumen de la historia

Tengo la mejor familia del mundo. Somos cincos personas en mi familia: mi padre, mi madre, mi hermano mayor, mi hermana y yo.

Mi padre, Guillermo, es médico. Trabaja en un hospital. Es muy bueno en su trabajo, pero debe trabajar en las noches y los fines de semana. Es muy divertido pero también es muy exigente sobre todo con nuestros estudios.

Mi madre, Sofia, es gerente de recursos humanos en una empresa. Ella es muy cariñosa y siempre nos cuida cuando nos sentimos mal. Ella trabaja de lunes a viernes. También es estricta al igual que mi padre.

Mi hermano mayor, Carlos, tiene dieciséis años. Es muy popular en la escuela. Le gusta mucho el deporte. Juega en el equipo de basquetbol de la escuela. Es un muy buen chico.

Mi hermana, Sofía, es una chica muy bonita, pero también es muy inteligente. Tiene quince años. También es popular y tiene muchos amigos. Ella es una persona muy cariñosa y amable con todos.

Luego, estoy yo. Tengo doce años. Me gustan los deportes, en particular, el béisbol. También me gusta mucho las clases de matemáticas y ciencias. Me gustaría ser astrofísico en el futuro.

Somos una familia pequeña, pero tengo dos tíos y cuatro tías, nueve primos, mis dos abuelitos y mis dos abuelitas. Cuando se une toda la familia, es una ocasión alegre y divertida.

Summary of the Story

I have the best family in the world. There are five people in my family: my father, my mother, my older brother, my sister, and me.

My father, Guillermo, is a doctor. He works in a hospital. He is very good at his job, but he must work at night and on weekends. He is very fun, but it is also very demanding, especially with our studies.

My mother, Sofia, is a human resources manager in a company. She is very affectionate and always takes care of us when we feel bad. She works from Monday to Friday. She is also strict, just like my father.

My older brother, Carlos, is sixteen. It is very popular in school. He likes sports a lot. He plays on the school basketball team. He is a very good boy.

My sister, Sofia, is a very pretty girl, but she is also very intelligent. She is fifteen years old. She is also popular and has many friends. She is a very affectionate and kind person with everyone.

Then, there's me. I'm twelve years old. I like sports, in particular, baseball. I also like math and science classes a lot. I would like to be an astrophysicist in the future.

We are a small family, but I have two uncles and four aunts, nine cousins, my two grandfathers, and two grandmothers. When the whole family gets together, it is a joyful and fun occasion.

Vocabulary

1. **mejor**	best
2. **de hecho**	in fact
3. **relativamente**	relatively
4. **no cabe duda**	no doubt
5. **sé**	I know
6. **porqué**	why
7. **buena pregunta**	good question
8. **para empezar**	to get started
9. **padre**	father
10. **atendiendo**	attending
11. **dedicado**	dedicated
12. **alegre**	cheerful
13. **divertida**	funny
14. **negativa**	negative
15. **estricto**	strict
16. **exigente**	demanding
17. **madre**	mother
18. **tierna**	tender
19. **cariñosa**	loving
20. **sufrir**	suffer
21. **hacernos**	make us
22. **sentir mejor**	feel better
23. **conscientes**	conscious
24. **buen comportamiento**	good behavior
25. **deportista**	athlete
26. **cerca**	near
27. **cualidades**	qualities

28. **brusco**	abrupt
29. **empuja**	push
30. **grita**	shouts
31. **lastimaría**	it would hurt
32. **bonita**	pretty
33. **sobre**	on
34. **contagiosa**	contagious
35. **cambiar de parecer**	change your mind
36. **nadie**	no one
37. **razonar**	to reason
38. **estrellas**	stars
39. **astronomía**	astronomy
40. **me gustaría**	I would like
41. **astrofísico**	astrophysicist
42. **tamaño**	size
43. **miembros**	members
44. **tíos**	uncles
45. **tías**	aunts
46. **primos**	cousins
47. **al final de cuentas**	in the end
48. **reunión**	meeting
49. **queremos**	we want
50. **apoyamos**	we support

Questions About the Story

1. ¿Cómo es mi familia?
    a. Es muy agresiva
    b. Es muy novedosa
    c. Es muy amplia
    d. Es muy pequeña
2. ¿Cuántos miembros hay en mi familia?
    a. Dos
    b. Tres
    c. Cuatro
    d. Cinco
3. ¿Cómo es mi hermano Carlos?
    a. Terrible
    b. Adorable
    c. Popular
    d. Tremendo
4. ¿Cómo es mi hermana Sofía?
    a. Terrible
    b. Tímida
    c. Tremenda
    d. Inteligente
5. ¿Cuántos primos tengo?
    a. Ocho

b. Nueve

c. Diez

d. Once

Answers

1. D
2. D
3. C
4. D
5. B

Chapter Twenty

Are You in Fashion? — ¿Estás a la moda?

El mundo de la moda es **cambiante**. Cada día, **surgen** nuevas ideas, nuevas **creaciones** y nuevas **tendencias**. Para las personas que les gusta estar a la **moda**, estar siempre a la moda es un **reto**. Es necesario conocer las nuevas tendencias en el **mundo** de la moda al igual que los **diseñadores** más populares del momento. Además, se debe conocer cuáles son las **marcas** más **influyentes** de la temporada **actual**.

Cuando se habla de moda, el punto **principal** es la ropa. La ropa es tan **amplia** y variada. Es realmente **difícil elegir** un solo **estilo**. De hecho, las personas que **disfrutan** de la moda siempre eligen varios estilos para usar según la ocasión.

Por ejemplo, existe **ropa formal**. Este estilo de vestir se usa en el trabajo o en **eventos formales**. En el trabajo, es común **vestir** formalmente especialmente cuando hay **reuniones de trabajo** con clientes o personas importantes. Para un hombre, el look **clásico** es un traje de **pantalón** y **saco** con **camisa** y **corbata**. Este look siempre va bien en cualquier situación.

En el caso de una mujer, un **atuendo formal** puede ser un traje formal, o bien, un vestido si se trata de un **evento social**. **Tradicionalmente**, se usa **vestido largo** para un evento formal y un **vestido corto** para un evento social. Claro, las reglas siempre se pueden **romper**.

Para vestir **diariamente**, las reglas cambian **drásticamente**. Se puede usar cualquier tipo de atuendo, según la ocasión y el clima. Cuando hace calor, es común usar ropa más fresca, es decir, ropa más fresca y de colores más claros. Las camisetas, playeras y pantalones cortos son muy populares. También se pueden usar vaqueros, aunque cuando hace mucho calor, no es muy buena idea.

Cuando hace frío, se debe usar ropa más **pesada** y de colores más o menos oscuros. Por ejemplo, se puede usar chaqueta, **suéter** o camisas y **blusas** de **manga larga**. En este caso, se usa ropa de **materiales** como la **lana** y el **algodón**. Son más calientes sobre todo cuando hace mucho aire o hasta nieve.

Luego, están los **accesorios**. Cuando se trata de accesorios, es un poco difícil saber por dónde empezar. La razón es porque hay tantos accesorios de dónde escoger. Por ejemplo, están las **joyas**, las gafas de sol, los relojes y los **collares**.

Los hombres, por lo regular, usan relojes y quizá una **cadena**. Las cadenas suelen ser de **oro** o de **plata**, dependiendo del gusto de la persona. Los relojes varían en **tamaño**, **estilo** y **precio**. Usualmente, un reloj es un accesorio que complementa el atuendo.

Entonces, es importante considerar el tamaño, color o cualquier otra función que éste tiene.

Las mujeres usan **aretes**, **sortijas**, **pulseras** o collares. Este tipo de joyas varían según el estilo y gusto de la persona. Usualmente, las joyas están hechas de oro o plata. Pero ahora se utilizan otro tipo de materiales como el plástico, la madera y hasta el cristal. En definitiva, el uso de los accesorios depende del atuendo y el look que la persona desea alcanzar.

Además, se debe considerar la marca y los precios de los artículos. Si una persona desea usar artículos de **marcas de lujo**, el **costo** de estos artículos tiende a ser muy alto. Entonces, es importante que considere si existe alguna otra marca más económica, o bien, se siente cómodo con el precio de los artículos.

Luego, existen algunas marcas y **casas de moda** que **promocionan** artículos para **consumo masivo**. Estas marcas no necesariamente son consideradas de lujo, pero tampoco son productos **baratos**. Esto significa que estos artículos son populares, pero son más económicos que las **versiones** de lujo. Son una muy buena **alternativa** para lucir bien, pero sin gastar mucho.

Finalmente, están los zapatos. Los zapatos son muy varios. Por ejemplo, las zapatillas deportivas son muy populares, y algunos estilos, también son muy costosos. En algunos casos, las zapatillas deportivas son más costosas que los zapatos de vestir de una casa de moda.

Para las mujeres existe una gran variedad de zapatos, **botas** y **sandalias**. Principalmente, existen zapatos de **tacón alto** y **tacón bajo**. También hay botas regulares y botas altas. Las sandalias son muy populares para un look **casual** o para un día muy caluroso.

Estar a la moda no es fácil porque requiere estar siempre informado sobre los cambios en las tendencias. Sin embargo, es una afición muy interesante y divertida.

Resumen de la historia

El mundo de la moda es cambiante. Para las personas que les gusta estar siempre a la moda, deben conocer sobre los cambios, innovaciones y tendencias. Para esto, deben estar informados sobre los nuevos estilos, diseñadores y marcas que surgen prácticamente a diario.

Primeramente, la ropa es lo más popular con respecto a la moda. Principalmente se tiene ropa formal y casual. La ropa formal se usa para el trabajo y los eventos formales. Un hombre puede usar un traje de pantalón y chaqueta con camisa y corbata. Una mujer puede usar un vestido largo o corto, según el tipo de evento queasiste.

Luego están los accesorios. Los accesorios pueden ser joyas como aretes, sortijas, pulseras y collares. El material más común para este tipo de accesorios es el oro y la plata. Ahora, existen otros materiales como el plástico, madera y cristal usado en los accesorios. Para los hombres, los relojes y las cadenas son accesorios comunes.

Cuando hace calor, ropa ligera y de colores claros es útil como playeras, camisetas y pantalones cortos. Cuando hace frío, ropa más pesada y de colores más oscuros son útiles. Los materiales de esta ropa son la lana y el algodón.

Finalmente, están los zapatos. Las zapatillas deportivas son muy populares, pero también son costosas. Luego, están los zapatos de tacón alto y tacón bajo. También son populares las botas.

Para estar a la moda, se requiere estar informado sobre los cambios en las tendencias de la moda. Es una afición divertida.

Summary of the Story

The world of fashion is changing. For people who like to be always in fashion, they should know about changes, innovations, and trends. Because of this, they must be informed about the new styles, designers, and brands that arise almost daily.

First, clothing is the most popular item with respect to fashion. Mainly, you have formal and casual clothes. Formal wear is used for work and formal events. A man can wear a suit consisting of trousers and a jacket with a shirt and tie. A woman can wear a long or short dress, depending on the type of event she attends.

Then there are the accessories. Accessories can be jewelry, such as earrings, rings, bracelets, and necklaces. The most common material for this type of accessories is gold and silver. Now, there are other materials, such as plastic, wood, and crystal used in the accessories. For men, watches and chains are common accessories.

On a hot weather, light and light-colored clothing, such as t-shirts, shirts, and shorts, are useful. When it's cold, heavier clothes and darker colors are useful. The materials of these clothes are wool and cotton.

Finally, there are the shoes. Sneakers are very popular, but they are also expensive. Then, there are high heels and low heels. Boots are also popular.

To be fashionable, it is necessary to be informed about changes in fashion trends. It is a fun hobby.

Vocabulary

1. **cambiante**	changing
2. **surgen**	arise
3. **creaciones**	creations
4. **tendencias**	trends
5. **moda**	fashion
6. **reto**	challenge
7. **mundo**	world
8. **diseñadores**	designers
9. **marcas**	brands
10. **influyentes**	influential
11. **actual**	current
12. **principal**	principal
13. **amplia**	wide
14. **difícil**	hard
15. **elegir**	to choose
16. **estilo**	style
17. **disfrutan**	enjoy
18. **ropa formal**	formal wear
19. **eventos formales**	formal events
20. **vestir**	wear
21. **reuniones de trabajo**	work meetings
22. **clásico**	classic
23. **pantalón**	trousers
24. **saco**	coat
25. **camisa**	shirt
26. **corbata**	tie

27. **atuendo formal**	formal attire
28. **evento social**	social event
29. **tradicionalmente**	traditionally
30. **vestido largo**	long dress
31. **vestido corto**	short dress
32. **romper**	to break
33. **diariamente**	daily
34. **drásticamente**	drastically
35. **pesada**	heavy
36. **suéter**	sweater
37. **blusas**	blouses
38. **manga larga**	long sleeve
39. **materiales**	materials
40. **lana**	wool
41. **algodón**	cotton
42. **accesorios**	accessories
43. **joyas**	jewelry
44. **collares**	necklaces
45. **cadena**	chain
46. **oro**	gold
47. **plata**	silver
48. **tamaño**	size
49. **estilo**	style
50. **precio**	price
51. **aretes**	earrings
52. **sortijas**	rings
53. **pulseras**	bracelets
54. **marcas de lujo**	luxury brands

55. **costo**	cost
56. **casas de moda**	fashion houses
57. **promocionan**	promote
58. **consumo masivo**	massive consume
59. **baratos**	cheap
60.**versiones**	versions
61. **alternativa**	alternative
62.**botas**	boots
63. **sandalias**	flips flops
64. **tacón alto**	high heel
65. **tacón bajo**	low heel
66. **casual**	casual

Questions About the Story

1. ¿Cómo es la moda?

    a. Divertida

    b. Interesante

    c. Estresante

    d. Cambiante

2. ¿Cuándo se usa la ropa formal?

    a. Para un evento casual

    b. Para una reunión

    c. Para una ir de compras

    d. Para una nueva fiesta

3. ¿Qué ropa se usa cuando hace calor?

    a. Camiseta y suéter

    b. Camiseta y pantalones cortos

    c. Playera y chaqueta formal

    d. Vaqueros y suéter

4. ¿Qué ropa se usa cuando hace frío?

    a. Camiseta y suéter

    b. Camiseta y pantalones cortos

    c. Playera y chaqueta formal

    d. Vaqueros y suéter

5. ¿Cuáles son accesorios?

    a. Zapatos y corbata

b. Joyas y relojes

c. Relojes y ropa

d. Collares y zapatos

Answers

1. D
2. B
3. B
4. D
5. B

Chapter Twenty-one:

Enjoying Good Music — Disfrutar de buena música

El mundo está lleno de música. En cualquier ciudad, o país, siempre se escucha música. No cabe duda de que la música es parte de la cultura e **identidad** de cada país, región y **etnia**. Cada **grupo social** tiene su propia música que le caracteriza. Esto es no sólo una expresión de su cultura e **identidad nacional**, sino que también es por el gusto de la buena música, la **diversión** y pasarla bien entre familia y amigos.

La música se caracteriza por el **ritmo** y la **melodía**. Todos los tipos de música tienen ritmo y melodía. Claro, éstos cambian según el tipo de música. Cuando la música es **alegre**, el ritmo es más rápido. Esto produce un ritmo que es muy bueno para bailar. Aunque no siempre debe ser rápida la música para **bailar**. En algunos casos, la música es un poco más **lenta**. Con esto, se pueden bailar ritmos diferentes de música.

Luego, la melodía cambia según el tipo de música. No importa si la música es para bailar, o solo para escucharla. La melodía crea el sonido que se percibe. **Por lo tanto**, una bonita melodía es agradable. Si la melodía no es agradable, entonces es muy probable que la música no cause agrado en las personas que la escuchan.

Para crear música, se utilizan **instrumentos musicales**. Hay todo tipo de instrumentos musicales. El instrumento más popular es el tambor. El **tambor** es un instrumento de **percusión**, es decir, se debe **golpear** con las **manos**, o con algún otro **dispositivo** para hacerlo **sonar**. Los tambores se usan en una gran variedad de estilos y géneros musicales. La función del tambor es marcar el ritmo de la música mientras que la melodía sigue el ritmo.

Otros instrumentos musicales son el **piano**, la **guitarra**, la **trompeta**, el **saxofón** o el **violín**. Todos estos instrumentos tienen diferentes **funciones** dentro de la música. Estos instrumentos pueden sonar al **mismo tiempo**, aunque cumplen con diversos momentos. Por ejemplo, la guitarra se usa para **marcar** ritmo, mientras que el saxofón usualmente lleva la melodía.

La música se divide en **piezas musicales**. La pieza musical más común es una **canción**. Una canción es una historia musical que representa las ideas y los **sentimientos** de los **compositores** y los **intérpretes**. Cuando se escribe una canción se tiene un estilo musical en mente. Por ejemplo, el estilo puede ser específicamente para el baile, o bien, para **relatar** una historia.

Los estilos musicales se conocen como **géneros**. Existen los géneros musicales son muy variados. Existen muchos estilos. Los estilos dependen de la cultura, región y **talentos** de los músicos que interpretan la música. Por ejemplo, si los músicos están entrenados en el estilo clásico, es común que interpreten música para **orquesta**. Esta música, conocida como música "clásica", tiene muchos años de existir. Es interpretada por miles de músicos en todas partes del mundo.

Otros estilos como el **rock**, **pop**, **salsa**, **merengue**, **blues** o **reggae** son géneros usualmente asociados con idiomas y las culturas que lo representan. En este sentido, es importante conocer las diferentes características de cada género. Algunos géneros solamente utilizan un tambor y las voces de los intérpretes. En otros casos, usan una serie de **arreglos** complejos como en el caso de una **sinfonía**. Otros tipos de música son completamente **electrónicos**, es decir, no utilizan instrumentos convencionales, sino que utilizan instrumentos eléctricos o sonidos generados por **computadoras**.

El único instrumento musical que no se ha podido replicar es la **voz humana**. La voz humana es única en cada persona. Cada individuo tiene su propia voz. Por eso es **virtualmente** imposible recrear los efectos de la voz humana. Aun cuando hay música totalmente electrónica, siempre se requiere del talento de una persona para **cantar**. "Cantar" es la acción de hacer melodías con la voz humana. Existen diferentes tipos de canto dentro de los cuales se destaca la **ópera**. La ópera es un género musical muy exigente para la voz de los **cantantes**.

Para disfrutar de la buena música no se necesita más que **amor** y gusto por la música. El género no importa. Lo que importa es tener el **deseo** de escuchar de una buena melodía y disfrutar de un buen ritmo para bailar. Los gustos dependen de cada persona. Así que no importan los gustos. Lo importante es disfrutar de todo tipo de música.

Resumen de la historia

La música se compone de dos elementos importantes, el ritmo y la melodía. El ritmo de la música es rápido o lento. Cuando la música es rápida, es ideal para bailar. Los ritmos para bailar se caracterizan por el uso del tambor. El tambor es un instrumento de percusión que se golpea con las manos o con otro dispositivo. Esto crea el ritmo.

La melodía se percibe conjuntamente con el ritmo. La melodía puede ser muy agradable o bien desagradable. Esto depende de los gustos de la persona que escucha la música. Si la persona no le gusta la melodía, esta resulta desagradable. Si le gusta la melodía, entonces es agradable.

La música se crea con instrumentos musicales. El tambor es un instrumento musical. Otros instrumentos musicales incluyen el piano, la guitarra, la trompeta, el saxofón y el violín. Estos son instrumentos utilizados en diferentes estilos musicales.

Los estilos musicales también se conocen como géneros. Los géneros son variados. Por ejemplo, está el rock, pop, salsa, merengue, reggae entre tantos otros. La música se divide en piezas musicales. La pieza más común es una canción. Una canción es una historia musical. Usualmente tiene una historia que contar.

El único instrumento musical que no se puede recrear es la voz humana. La voz humana es única para cada individuo. Por eso es virtualmente imposible crearla con una computadora.

El gusto por la buena música no importa del género sino del buen gusto de cada persona.

Summary of the Story

Music is composed of two important elements, rhythm, and melody. The rhythm of music is either fast or slow. When the music is fast, it is ideal for dancing. The rhythms to dance are characterized by the use of the drum. The drum is a percussion instrument that is struck with the hands or with another device. This creates the rhythm.

Melody is perceived along with the rhythm. The melody can be very pleasant or unpleasant. This depends on the taste of the person who listens to music. If the person does not like the melody, it is unpleasant. If they like the melody, then it's nice.

Music is created with musical instruments. The drum is a musical instrument. Other musical instruments include piano, guitar, trumpet, saxophone, and violin. These are instruments used in different musical styles.

Musical styles are also known as genres. The genres are varied. For example, there is rock, pop, salsa, merengue, reggae, among many others. Music is divided into musical pieces. The most common piece is a song. A song is a musical story. It usually has a story to tell.

The only musical instrument that cannot be recreated is the human voice. The human voice is unique to each individual. That is why it is virtually impossible to create it with a computer.

The taste for good music does not depend on the genre but on the good taste of each person.

Vocabulary

1. **identidad**	identity
2. **etnia**	ethnicity
3. **grupo social**	social group
4. **identidad nacional**	national identity
5. **diversión**	fun
6. **ritmo**	rhythm
7. **melodía**	melody
8. **alegre**	cheerful
9. **bailar**	dance
10. **lenta**	slow
11. **por lo tanto**	thus
12. **instrumentos musicales**	musical instruments
13. **tambor**	drum
14. **percusión**	percussion
15. **golpear**	hit
16. **manos**	hands
17. **dispositivo**	device
18. **sonar**	sound
19. **piano**	piano
20. **guitarra**	guitar
21. **trompeta**	trumpet
22. **saxofón**	saxophone
23. **violín**	fiddle
24. **funciones**	functions
25. **mismo tiempo**	same time
26. **marcar**	mark

27. **piezas musicales**	pieces musicals
28. **canción**	song
29. **sentimientos**	feelings
30. **compositores**	composers
31. **intérpretes**	interpreters
32. **relatar**	tell
33. **géneros**	genders
34. **talentos**	talents
35. **orquesta**	orchestra
36. **rock**	rock
37. **pop**	pop
38. **salsa**	sauce
39. **merengue**	meringue
40. **blues**	blues
41. **reggae**	reggae
42. **arreglos**	arrangements
43. **sinfonía**	symphony
44. **electrónicos**	electronic
45. **computadoras**	computers
46. **voz humana**	human voice
47. **virtualmente**	virtually
48. **cantar**	to sing
49. **ópera**	opera
50. **cantantes**	singers
51. **amor**	love
52. **deseo**	wish

Question About the Story

1. ¿Cómo se llaman los estilos musicales?
    a. Ritmo
    b. Melodía
    c. Forma
    d. Género
2. ¿Cuáles son los dos elementos de la música?
    a. Ritmo y melodía
    b. Tambor y piano
    c. Voz y talento
    d. Instrumento y voz
3. ¿Cuáles son los instrumentos musicales?
    a. Ritmo, piano ytambor
    b. Tambor, piano yviolín
    c. Melodía, saxofón y género
    d. Piano, melodía y ritmo
4. ¿Cuál es el mejor ejemplo de una piezamusical?
    a. Género
    b. Canción
    c. Forma
    d. Estilo
5. ¿Cuál es el instrumento musical que no se puede replicar?
    a. Voz humana

b. Voz electrónica

c. Voz encantada

d. Voz iluminada

Answers

1. D
2. A
3. B
4. B
5. A

Conclusion

Thank you for making it all the way to the end of this book. If you have made it this far, it is because you are committed to improving your Spanish skills. You are not only determined to make an effort, but you are also willing to see it through to the end.

So, what's next?

Please go back and review any stories where you would like to get more practice on. It is always a good idea to go back and review vocabulary, as you might discover something new.

Also, take the time to read the stories aloud. This will help you practice pronunciation and begin improving your overall speaking fluency. In addition, try out the language, which you have learned in this book, with any Spanish-speaking friends you may have. You will notice that it isn't as hard as you might have thought to communicate with them.

Above all, keep in mind that practice makes perfect. So, the more you practice, the more you will be able to improve on your current skills. If you can dedicate a few minutes of your day every day to the study of Spanish, you will soon find that your skills have improved. The biggest effect of this improvement will be your self-confidence gaining momentum.

Thank you once again for reading this book. We hope it has been useful and informative and that it has been worth your while. Keep up the good work!

www.ingramcontent.com/pod-product-compliance
Lightning Source LLC
Chambersburg PA
CBHW080847190726
48292CB00010B/2902
9781951764470